LIVING YOUR PURPOSE

RICK GREEN

Mike,
Live it!
— [signature]

For additional copies of this book or for more information on other books, contact:

Revolutionary Strategies
P.O. Box 900
Dripping Springs, TX 78620
(512) 858-0974
www.RickGreen.com

Cover design:
Ashley Franks

Printed in the United States of America
ISBN 978-0-9883527-5-9

DEDICATION
Zig Ziglar & Dr. Charles Jarvis

Other than my father, Mr. Ziglar and Dr. Jarvis taught me more about success and purpose than anyone on the planet. And since they were the sources of most of what dad taught me as well, that makes them the two main influences for the success principles I share in this book.

Even as I was writing this book, Mr. Ziglar & Dr. Jarvis both went home to glory in the span of just a few weeks. I am so thankful for their friendship, mentorship, and counsel over the years. When I spoke at Dr. Jarvis' "celebration of life" (no funerals here!) I promised his family that his jokes and stories would live on as long as I could get away with telling them in my speeches!

Gentlemen, thank you for finding your passion, fulfilling your purpose, and inspiring so many millions of us to do the same.

CONTENTS

PASSION

PURPOSE

PREFACE
by Kara Green

I am excited that you have chosen to take on the challenge of *Living Your Purpose*. I believe the tools you will learn as you work through the pages of this book are going to prove to be one of the best investments you have ever made. I say this with absolute confidence because over the last twenty years I have watched my husband, Rick Green, as he has implemented these strategies in his personal and professional life. I know first hand that they work and if you allow me a little latitude to brag on my husband, I think you will agree that the results in his life have been pretty remarkable.

- Rick graduated from college in two years, with a four-year degree.
- At the age of twenty he enrolled in one of the nation's top law schools.
- At the ripe old age of twenty-six he ran for and won a seat in the Texas Legislature.
- Over the years he has built several successful companies, some even while still in law school.
- Today he is a nationally recognized speaker, author, and radio host, and reaches hundreds of thousands of people each year through live audience events, and millions more through radio and television.
- Rick is the Founder and President of the elite youth

leadership program in the nation, Patriot Academy.

- He accomplished all of his successes while also coaching his sons' baseball teams, and not losing sight of his top priorities—faith and family.

One of the reasons that Rick has been able to accomplish so much in such a short period of time, while still maintaining his sanity, health, and commitment to faith and family, is largely due to the strategies he outlines in this book. These principles have become disciplines in his life, enabling him both to discover his God-given mission and to stay on track with that purpose and plan.

Over the last eleven years, Rick has been equipping future leaders of America through Patriot Academy, a six-day political leadership program. Part of the training that the students receive includes teaching them how to implement these strategies into their lives. In this book, Rick lays out these same life principles with the hope that many more will be successful in fulfilling the purpose that God intended for their lives. I have no doubt that if that is your desire, this book will give you the necessary tools to begin *Living Your Purpose*.

INTRODUCTION

Getting Started

Let me start by saying that I have not discovered a new formula for success that has never been known to man before. I am not a "success guru." In fact, nothing in this book is really new at all—the opposite is actually true. A long time ago I was taught an ancient biblical truth from the writings of the wisest man who ever lived, King Solomon. I believe the words he wrote, with all my heart:

> *That which has been is what will be, that which is done is what will be done, and there is nothing new under the sun.* - **Ecclesiastes 1:9**

I am not a modern day sage. What I am, is an avid student of history—or as King Solomon would say, a student of *that which has been.*

I love reading biographies of men and women who against all odds, have lived with passion and achieved their goals. By studying the lives of those who radically changed their world, I have observed firsthand the veracity of King Solomon's words. The same life principles, which enabled those who have gone before us to live their purpose, will also help us to do the same today. These principles truly are nothing new. In fact, they are virtually universal and timeless strategies that will benefit us when we apply them to our lives. What's more, I have found that they are principles that are almost always missing in the lives of those who, in the words of Henry David Thoreau are living, *"Lives of quiet desperation."*

Living Your Purpose is my way of sharing some of the processes that have worked best in my own life. My goal is not to create a new system, but to simply pass along what I have found to be some of the most effective principles I have learned. Throughout the pages of this book, I will share a number of "golden nuggets" that I have gleaned from others, such as, Zig Ziglar, Dr. Charles Jarvis, Krish Dhanam, John Maxwell, Paul Tsika, and even my own father, Richard Green, Sr. My prayer is that working through the concepts in these pages will help you to discover how to live your life for the Lord with passion and purpose.

How to Use This Book

Although I arranged the chapters in the order that I believe is best to lead you through the process of discovering and living your purpose, undoubtedly, some chapters may not apply to your specific situation. Ultimately, this is your life plan so the beauty of this process is that you can follow through chapter by chapter and build your plan, or you can skip around and focus on those chapters that you believe will best help you discover your passion and accomplish your goals. The choice is yours.

At the end of each chapter are questions designed to help you apply and work through the principles in the material you just read. The questions will draw out the desires of your heart. They will help you define your passion and purpose and see your strengths and hindrances more clearly.

Some space is provided in this book for you to write in, initially. However, I would suggest keeping a separate journal or creating a document on your computer so you will be able to add to and rework your answers, as you proceed with this process. If you purchased this book with the CD Set and digital workbook, you might want to answer all of the questions in digital format on your computer or through your handheld device so you do not have to go back and type in your handwritten answers. Some people prefer to first work through this process the old fashioned way, with pen and paper. I must admit that there is still something inspiring and poetic about the actual written word.

Regardless of whether you write in digital format or even go all the way back to feathered pen and ink well, you should think of this as an opportunity for you to write your own book—your personal life plan—because that is essentially what you will be doing. Answer each question as best you can, but your answers don't have to be perfect. This is not for others to read, it is your own private life plan and you will be refining it over the weeks, months, and years to come.

The method that has worked best for me as I've developed my life plan over the past two decades is to quickly answer the questions in the chapters that I read each day, and then come back and review what I wrote every week or two. In that way, by the time I get to the end of the book, I have answered all the questions and gone through my entire life planning process a number of times. If you're like me, you may end up with 100-150 pages or more.

Make a goal of reading fifteen to twenty pages in your life plan every day. This way you will be going back over the same material and fine-tuning your answers every week or two. This process will help you become more focused and will also help you to discover, on a daily basis, those things that will need to be changed in a particular area.

For instance, maybe you will be working on the goals for your physical life and your plan for getting in shape and living a healthier life and you will find that it affects goals you have in other areas. Or, maybe you decide to make a change with your speaking introduction because you find that there is something in your life that inspires other people and you want to include it your introduction. You'll see those things more and more, as you get into the process on a consistent basis.

The point is, throughout this entire process you are going to be changing your personal life plan, so don't think it has to be perfect the first time around. I change mine all the time. Some areas become more concrete as you go along, others will grow less important. It is a flexible process.

Working with your life plan is something that you want to establish as a habit in your life. Every morning, take a little time either during your prayer and devotions, or as a separate activity that you set aside time for, before you start your day. You should purpose to spend at least fifteen to twenty minutes working on your life plan each day.

The Beginning of a Lifestyle

This is an ongoing process. You might complete a particular chapter each day, or you may decide to work on it for 20 minutes and go as far as you can in that time. If you are like me, you may find that whenever you have a few minutes you are jumping in and working on it. Whatever you decide to do, the key is to continue in the process as often as you can. The more you work through your life plan, the more likely you will stay on task and not be distracted by things that are not aligned with your passion and purpose. In that way, you will ensure that the good things in life will not take away from the great things.

The fact that you are reading this book is a pretty good indication you are a person who wants to be a difference maker. One of the biggest challenges for people like us is that we always have lots of people pulling us in different directions. Opportunities are always coming our way, and we need to be able to identify those things that will keep us on track and enable us to fulfill our purpose. That is what this life plan will help you to do.

Should Christians Set Goals and Make Plans?

I have a couple of thoughts to share with you before you dive in and begin discovering your passion and planning your purpose. You might find yourself asking along the way, why it is so important to make plans anyway. After all, isn't it true that whatever is going to happen, is just going to happen? If God is sovereign, then why should we concern ourselves with planning out the things that we want to do?

Colossians 3:23 is one of the driving verses of my life and really has helped answer that question for me.

Whatever you do, do it heartily, as to the Lord and not to men. - **Colossians 3:23**

The idea is that you work as hard as you can, to be the best that you can be, not for personal gain or to have your name in lights, but to do it as unto the Lord and not unto men. This means you do your best with the talents and skills that God has given you. This is the verse I use when coaching my son's baseball team. I have the opportunity to work with these kids on the baseball field and remind them that everything they do, they are to do to the best of their ability, as unto God.

Another Scripture that inspires me is a parable that Jesus taught his disciples, the parable of the talents in Matthew 25. Here we learn about three servants who were each given talents. When the master went away, he expected them to use and multiply those talents. Two of them did exactly that, and they were given even more responsibility when the master returned. However, one of them buried the talent and when the master came back he said that servant was wicked and slothful. We don't want to be in that position one day. We want to be the ones who are making the most of what God has given to us.

That's what planning in your life is all about. It's about taking inventory of the unique talents, abilities, and opportunities that God has given you, and living out the purpose for which He has created you. It is your responsibility to take all that He has given you, and do your best to live out His purposes for your life.

As you make your goals and plans, one other verse to keep in mind is from the Book of James. It says,

> *Come now, you who say, "Today or tomorrow we will go to such and such a city, spend a year there, buy and sell, and make a profit"; whereas you do not*

know what will happen tomorrow. For what is your life? It is even a vapor that appears for a little time and then vanishes away. Instead you ought to say, "If the Lord wills, we shall live and do this or that." But now you boast in your arrogance. All such boasting is evil. Therefore, to him who knows to do good and does not do it, to him it is sin. - **James 4:13-17**

To me that verse means that while God does expect us to work hard, make plans, and do our best to fulfill those plans, we must always keep the perspective that we will do those things only, *"If the Lord wills."* So, when I make my plans and set my goals every morning, I always say, *"Lord willing."* I do that to remind myself that it is only if it is God's will for my life that I want to go in that direction. I know that He has put certain things on my heart, and given me a passion to do them, and at some point, I do believe that it will be His will for me to march forward in them, unless He shows me in some way that it is not His will.

The point is balance. I don't believe that as a person of faith you should sit back and say, "whatever is going to happen is going to happen," but I also don't believe that we should strive in a way that we believe we can *make* our goals happen regardless of God's Will. I think we have to have a balanced perspective. Lord willing, we will go and do those things that He has placed on our hearts. We will work at it to the best of our abilities and with all of our hearts, as Colossians says. But we will do it with the recognition that

God is sovereign and if His will is something totally different, that is what we want. We don't want to be working for something that is good, if takes us away from God's perfect will for our lives.

In my case, I've run for state political office several times, winning several times and losing others. Today I look back and realize that had I won some of the races that I lost, I would have been stuck in a position that would have prevented me from being able to do some of the most fun, amazing things that God has allowed me to do over the last few years.

So just know there is a balance. God has a plan for your life and He expects you to work the plan. You must desire *His* plan, and then live it to the best of your ability. Remember what Proverbs 16:9 says:

A man's heart plans his way, but the LORD directs his steps.

About this passage, Matthew Henry wrote this in his commentaries:

Man is here represented to us, 1. As a reasonable creature, that has the faculty of contriving for himself: His heart devises his way, designs an end, and projects ways and means leading to that end, which the inferior creatures, who are governed by sense and natural instinct, cannot do. The more shame for him if he does not devise the way how to please God and provide for his everlasting state. 2. But as a depending creature, that is subject to the direction and dominion of his Maker. If men devise their way, so as to make God's glory their end and his will their rule, they may expect that he will direct their steps by his Spirit and grace, so that they shall not miss their way nor come short of their end. But let men devise their worldly affairs ever so politely, and with ever so great a probability of success, yet God has the ordering of the event, and sometimes directs their steps to that which they least intended. The design of this is to teach us to say, If the Lord will, we shall live and do this or that (James 4:14, 15), and to have our eye to God, not only in the great turns of our lives, but in every step we take. Lord, direct my way, 1 Thessalonians 3:11.

I think that sums it up. If we are doing our duty, then we are planning our lives and working hard to make the most of what we have been given. We are doing it in a way that respects and honors God's sovereignty, while allowing Him to order the events and direct our steps. That is why we need to be flexible.

Constantly reviewing your life plan will make sure you are staying within your greatest purpose, as well as being sensitive to God's leading in your life.

There are seasons for everything. So it doesn't mean that you may be in the same job or career for your whole life. Your purpose may have you in a particular area or career at one time, and then God will move you and direct your steps into another area later in life. If you had not experienced the first job, you may not have been prepared for what came next. God uses all of those things in our lives. As Romans 8:28 says,

> *All things work together for good to those who love God,*
> *to those who are the called according to His purpose.*

Everything you have done until now is preparing you for the things that God is going to have you do in the future. The purpose of this book is to help you identify and discover that passion and effectively live your purpose.

Standing on the Shoulders of Giants

I want to say one final thing about those mentors who I have learned from in the past. Throughout this book, I will be using bits and pieces of information that I have gleaned from them as I have been developing this life planning process over the past ten years. I have to confess, the lines have blurred between what are my own original thoughts and what came from others. I've done my best to credit all the actual quotes and any specific processes that I know came from others, but I'm asking them, and you, to forgive me if I miss one. I say all that because as you begin this journey I want you to know that you are standing on the shoulders of giants.

With that said, it is time for you to get started *Living Your Purpose*!

Rick Green

IDENTITY

1
RESPONSIBILITY = POWER!

Do you know what God has put you on this earth to accomplish? Most people don't. To live your purpose, you must know what that purpose is. The goal of this book is to help you discover and fulfill the unique plan for which God has created you.

As you work through these first four chapters in this section of the book you will be focusing on your identity. How do you identify yourself today? Do you know why you do the things you do? Your beliefs about who you are directly affect the choices you make. So, knowing what those beliefs are and where they came from is essential. The reason so many people never fulfill their purpose is because they have the wrong identity of themselves. They have given the control of their lives to others, and have allowed past circumstances to determine who they are and what they will do.

In order to live your purpose you need to have an empowered identity. An empowered identity simply means that you assume responsibility for the outcome of your life. You no longer allow circumstances and other people to define who you are and what you do. In this chapter you will learn how to identify and take responsibility for the things that happen to you, and how to respond to your circumstances in a way that enables you to influence the direction of your life.

The Blame Game

Believe me, there is no one on the planet more responsible for the results of your life than you.

Now, that may sound obvious. You are the one who makes the decisions so of course you are ultimately responsible for the outcome of those choices. However, in reality, we live in a society that promotes just the opposite mentality. The majority of our culture today is increasingly unwilling to own up to their choices and decisions. The message that is continually reinforced is that personal success or failure lies in the hands of others—our parents, our teachers, our elected officials. The popular thing to do in America today is to look for someone else to blame when things go wrong.

How many times have you heard a person excuse their actions due to some past circumstance? Maybe it was the way their parents treated them when they were younger, or the neighborhood they grew up in, or the school they attended, or any host of other imperfect circumstances they have allowed to control them and define their identity.

When a business fails, the blame is often laid on the competition, employees, or the economy. We even see this blame game in the office of the President of the United States, who quickly points the finger at the previous administration rather than assuming responsibility for the direction of this nation under his leadership. We have indeed become a society of blame shifters—we are always looking for someone else to blame for the outcome of our choices.

We all know the term "dysfunctional family." Can anyone show me a functional family? Every family has problems. Every child disagrees with their parents, and at some point in all of our lives bad things happen to us that we wish had never occurred. But in our society today criminals are being set free, children are going undisciplined, and guilty employees are being held blameless. We allow them to excuse their current actions on account of some past event that happened in their lives.

Regardless of how big or small a circumstance in your past may be, if you use it as an excuse for your current actions and situation, you are actually diminishing the power of your life by giving it over to others. Casting blame may relieve you of the burden of responsibility for the outcome of your life, and this may feel good for the moment. But when you shift the blame, you are actually giving up the power to be able to change your circumstances and improve your life, thereby moving forward. When we do this, we are acting like powerless victims who have no control over the outcome of our lives.

Yet, countless others who have faced similar

circumstances, or even worse, have chosen a different response. They have not allowed it to control their lives. They have never cast blame, committed a heinous crime, or been a drain on society because of the unfortunate events in their past. I believe that one of the reasons we are seeing a "lack of responsibility" mentality increasing in our society today stems from the fact that we are constantly encouraged to lean on the government. We think the government should take responsibility for the outcome of our lives. We want guaranteed jobs and guaranteed health care. We want someone else to do the things that we should be willing to do for ourselves.

If you find that you are blaming the government, other people, or past circumstances for the current condition of any area of your life, whether it is physical, spiritual, financial, mental, or in your relationships with others, you have completely disempowered yourself. You have no power to make a change or improve that area of your life because you have given the control over to others. Whoever you have given the responsibility to is the one who has the power over the situation.

When you blame others for things they have done to you in the past, it prevents you from moving forward and being able to change what needs to be changed. By holding them responsible, you have given them the power and control over that area of your life.

Mixed Signals

As an illustration, I want you to imagine for a moment that you are behind the steering wheel of a car. You are in the driver's seat, but your hands are tied and you are not controlling the steering wheel. Your spouse is in the passenger seat and has a little box that controls the steering. Your parents are in the back seat (whether they are still living or not) and one of them is controlling the break while the other has the gearshift. Your employer has his foot on the gas pedal, and your kids have the emergency break.

What's going to make this trip interesting is not so much that you are not in control, but the fact that everyone in the car is acting independently. Your wife is trying to turn you to the right, your employer is putting the pedal to the metal, your kids are slamming on the emergency brake, and your mom is shifting into reverse. This would be an insane car ride, correct? Yet, that is exactly how most people live their lives every day.

By blaming other people and past circumstances for the results of their current actions, they have given the control of that area of their lives over to others. If you get nothing else out of this book I pray you remember this, *"It is not what happens to you, it's what you do with what happens to you that matters most."*

The Ultimate Comeback Kid

My mom always told me, *"Do the best you can with what you got, right where you are."* One of the best examples of someone who did this throughout his life is Joseph, in the Old Testament. His response to the life changing circumstances that came into his life, unexpectedly, reveals the exact kind of mentality we need to adopt in our lives as well.

Consider the remarkable events of his story. When he was a teen, his own brothers tried to kill him and then settled for selling him into slavery. Instead of whining and crying and feeling sorry for himself, he did the best he could with what he was given. By choosing to respond in that way, his talents and willingness to be used by God found him favor. In time, his master entrusted his entire household into his care.

He undoubtedly had a great attitude. A man of influence like Joseph's Master would not promote a servant who was whining and crying about their circumstances. I would imagine Joseph gave every task his absolute best and even did so with a smile on his face, spreading joy with an infectious optimism to those around him.

Then one day his master's wife lied to her husband about Joseph and he was stripped of his duties and thrown into jail. Once again, Joseph found himself in a devastating situation. He had been falsely accused, yet he chose to do the best he could with what he had been given. There is no record of him whining or complaining or feeling sorry for himself. Instead, he became obedient to those in authority over him. He must have once again given every task his absolute best and infused those around him with joyful work ethic because the warden soon put him in charge of the entire jail.

Joseph's next promotion was better than taking over Apple Computer or even Chick-fil-a. Upon release from prison, he was put in charge of the entire nation of Egypt. He was second only to Pharaoh himself. This was not like a ceremonial vice-president attending state funerals and hosting entertainers at the White House. Joseph was the Chief Operating Officer of the most powerful nation on the planet.

A great famine hit the land, but Joseph's wise stewardship saved Egypt and surrounding nations, even including his own brothers who came to him for food. When they realized the man they were dealing with was their brother Joseph, who they had sold into slavery, they were afraid for their lives. But Joseph's response proved that they were not in control of his life. He told them that what they had meant for evil God had meant for good.

Joseph could have lived a very different life. He could have easily sat around and complained about how tough and unfair his life had been. He could have blamed his brothers and his master's wife for the problems he had. He could have complained to God about everything always going against him. He had some pretty good reasons to complain and be bitter, but he chose not to focus on what happened to him. Instead, he looked for ways to bring God the glory, wherever he was. As a result, the entire world was saved from starvation.

Not bad for a little fella born to an extremely dysfunctional family from the wrong side of the tracks.

It's Your Choice

Just like Joseph, you have a choice about how you will respond to the things that happen to you. You can blame someone else for your problems and be miserable, or you can take responsibility and do the best you can with what you have been given. Choosing to take responsibility regardless of how you got into the situation you are in will empower you to make changes, improve your life, and bring glory to God.

Do you want to be miserable for the rest of your life? If so, there's a real simple formula. Just keep blaming everybody else for all the problems you have. If you would rather become empowered beyond your wildest dreams, begin by acknowledging that God is in control—not the events of your past. He has given you the power to choose how you will respond, and to take the necessary actions that will determine your outcome.

One of the underlying belief systems necessary for you to live your purpose is the belief that you have the ability to affect your future. Whether you realize it or not, you have the ability to impact how your current situations will affect your outcome. Once you willingly accept responsibility for your life and recognize that you are not just a puppet controlled by the forces around you, your life will be empowered as you begin to influence the outcome.

Faith AND Action!

This approach does not at all mean you are doing this on your own like the New Age and Self-Help gurus who would make you out to be "like God" and in control of everything all by yourself. One can easily swing between the extremes of either thinking you are a god and controlling the outcome, or doing absolutely nothing because you expect God to do everything for you.

In *Living Your Purpose*, we are attempting a balanced approach wherein you are using the tools God gave you, rather than being the "wicked and slothful" servant who buried his talent. An empowered identity is simply a matter of you obeying the Biblical commands to be transformed by the renewing of your mind and make sure there is some action to go along with your faith.

There are three kinds of people in the world. There are those that make things happen, those that watch what happens, and those that wonder what in the world happened. Which one of those three will you be? It's entirely your choice. The first thing you have to do is accept responsibility for doing the best you can with whatever has happened to you. Once you acknowledge that it's not what happens to you, but what you do with what happens to you, your hands are going to be back on the steering wheel of your life. You will break those chains that were holding you in bondage while everyone else was making the decisions and controlling the outcome of your life. Once you break those chains and accept responsibility, you dramatically increase your ability to be used in an unlimited way.

One of the major goals of this book is to encourage you to not only accept responsibility, but also to do it with enthusiasm. Be excited about the fact that you can look back at those things in your past and say, *"Yes, some bad things happened to me, things that I didn't want to have happen, things that I could have done differently, and some things that were totally outside of my control. But I can control my response today and take back the steering wheel of my life."*

As we delve deeper into your identity, you will begin answering some questions about your beliefs regarding past situations and how you have defined those events. You will discover areas where you may have given others too much control by blaming them for the things that happened to you. The reason you are going through this exercise is not so you can pile up regrets, but so you can acknowledge the fact that you do have influence and impact on the things that happen to you. You do not have to be a victim or a bystander any longer. You are an active participant in your life, and it is time to begin taking back the control from others.

As you go through this process, you are going to ask

yourself if there is anything that you can do right now to improve the situation. If you can't think of anything, you are lying to yourself. There is always something you can do to improve. Most people simply react to everything that happens to them and as a result, they get pushed and pulled and controlled by the events and people around them.

When you act instead of react, you will begin to move purposely towards your desired outcome and won't be led around aimlessly by circumstances. Steven Covey calls it being proactive. Zig Ziglar calls it responding. It simply means you adding your influence to the situation, rather than being powerless.

Most go through life letting circumstances control their direction, attitude, and outcome. When they don't make the team or get the job, they decide to give up. They say things like, "*I guess it just wasn't meant be.*" Do you think great leaders like Abraham Lincoln, Vince Lombardy, Beethoven, or Walt Disney allowed other people to control their outcome? Do you think they blamed others when things didn't go their way? I don't. I think they accepted responsibility for the part they could play in the outcome, and as a result they fulfilled their dreams.

These men were all told by "experts" that they would never make it, that they didn't have what it took to succeed in their fields. But they met every trial with sheer determination and instead of letting the circumstances control their outcome, they responded proactively and that took them in their desired direction.

Some of you may think, "*I am not supposed to be in the driver's seat, God is.*" All I can say to that argument is what a traffic jam there would be if everyone hopped into the passenger seat of their actual cars and asked God to do all the driving.

The same is true as we travel along the road of life. Yes, God is in control, but He drives through you and me. He uses us to make an impact on the world for Him. He tells us where to go and what to do, but we have to listen to His instructions and do the driving. Should we not get out a map and plot a course for the destination to which He has called us?

It is *your* responsibility to work on the desires of your heart—no one else can do that for you. As you acknowledge God's sovereignty in your life, and make and execute the plans He has for you, you will begin to fulfill your purpose and honor Him in the process. By doing everything as unto the Lord and not unto men, you will stay within His perfect plan for your life.

That is the reason for the exercises in which you are about to engage. By constantly analyzing and reassessing whether or not you are where God wants you to be, you are making sure to keep in touch with the Master Planner. The idea is not to remove God from the equation and go it alone, but to ask Him to use you more. By being willing to follow His instructions, instead of being led by random events and people, you will be doing what God Has called you to do and not allowing others to control your destiny.

I believe God gives each of us the choice of whether or not we are going to serve him and fulfill our greatest purposes. Below are three scenarios—you decide which outcome you would prefer.

Scenario One:

Imagine for the next twenty years you allow the circumstances that occur to control the direction and outcome of your life. All the while you watch, wishing you could do something about it, but with no power to change anything. What would it feel like to look back at your life after twenty years of being blown around by the winds of circumstance? Do you think you would have regrets? How about unfulfilled dreams and hopes? Do you think you would wish that your life had gone in a different direction? Would you resent the fact that other people had too much control over the outcome of your life? Would you resent yourself for not stepping up and responding differently, so that the outcome would have been better? If you knew that would be the scenario for you for the next twenty years, would you be excited about what the future holds? How does it feel to consider living the next twenty years without accepting responsibility for the outcome of your life?

Scenario Two:

Imagine for the next twenty years you live with an attitude that ignorance is bliss. You don't want to know or worry about where you are going to be in the future, or how you are going to get there. Twenty years from now, what do you think it will feel like to suddenly wake up and wonder how in the world you ended up where you are? Will you regret that you didn't take responsibility for the direction of your life? How do you think it will feel in twenty years to wish you were somewhere completely different? Do you think you will regret letting twenty years of your life go by without any focus, direction, or true accomplishment? You sat back in your "ignorance is bliss" attitude and wasted twenty years of your life. Worst of all, how do you think it will feel to realize that you didn't fulfill your God-given purpose, to know that you missed out on His perfect will for your life just because you did not want to take responsibility.

The Third Option (a great Vince Flynn novel, by the way)

I don't like either of those twenty-year scenarios, and I'm sure you agree. Now take a look at scenario three and see if it is a bit more appealing.

Scenario Three:

Imagine if right now, today, you stop complaining about circumstances and wishing things were different, and you immediately start taking control of your life. First, you set out to determine to know God's purposes for you, and then you commit to doing whatever it takes to fulfill His plans. Now, what do you think your life will look like in twenty years? What will you accomplish for the Lord? How do you think it will feel to know that for the past twenty years you implemented the strategies and responses necessary to accept responsibility for the things (both good and bad) that occurred in your life? How do you think it will feel to know that you always did your best with what you had been given? What do you think your relationships with God and others will look like? Where do you think you will be in twenty years if you let God use you for His glory and His kingdom?

What will your life look like if for the next twenty years you are constantly improving and working harder for the Lord?

Regardless of where you are today, I think you would agree with me that *Scenario Three* is the place you would like to be in twenty years. However, the sad reality is not every one of us will be there. It's totally your choice, it is entirely up to you. You have one life to give. The question posed by this book is: for what will you give your one life? Are you willing to give it your best? Are you willing to live your purpose? Don't wait twenty years to decide.

Do it now.

Today is the day to begin and it starts with taking responsibility.

Work through the following questions and start writing the book of your life—your masterpiece.

1. Who on this planet is most responsible for the results of your life?

2. List at least three situations in your life that you currently "blame" someone else for and then ask the questions below about each.

   1.

   2.

   3.

3. Was there anything at all that YOU could have done different that might have changed the outcome?

4. Is there ANYTHING at all that you can personally do to improve this situation now?

5. What has to happen for you to accept responsibility, and therefore get the power, in each of these situations?

6. What specific action steps can you take to accept responsibility in these areas?

7. Responsibility = POWER! Explain what that means.

If you accept responsibility you will have the power to change your life.

When you claim the captain's chair in your life, amazing things will happen.

2

HOW DO YOU SEE YOURSELF?

Have you ever known a person who was incredibly successful, yet despite all that success wound up sabotaging themselves, and losing everything? How about someone who seems to have every opportunity in the world drop right into his or her lap, but for some reason they are never able to catch a break? What about the person who, despite great obstacles and against all odds, successfully overcomes and fulfills their purpose? Would it surprise you to know that the underlying reason for each of these results in a person's life boils down to one primary ingredient—the way they see themselves.

It's true. One of the greatest influences in your life is your own definition of who you are. It is a powerful factor and something you have complete control over. How you view yourself directly influences the actions, attitudes, and outcomes of your life.

So, how do you see yourself? And *why* do you see yourself in that way?

Everything that happens in your life is processed through the mental filter of your identity. For instance, if you did not identify yourself as a child of God, then you would not understand the many ways in which He could bless your life. That one change in your definition of who you are would drastically alter every other area of your life.

Identity Crisis

What's amazing is that most people pay very little attention to how their personal identity is formed. They never actually think about how they view themselves, or if they would like to make a change. This lack of personal identity is responsible for most of our societal problems. Take a look at our youth today—very few of them know whom they are. Most don't feel good about themselves. They follow other kids around at school trying to fit in. They are even grasping to understand their own gender identity, as nobody seems to know what the roles are for men and women anymore.

One of my favorite books is *Tender Warrior*, by Stu Webber. It's a classic that I recommend to everyone. I even gave a copy of it to all the guys in my wedding party twenty years ago. It was written in 1993, but it is as relevant today as it was then. Here's a quote he uses in the book, from a Garrison Keller article:

This was not a great year for guys. Guys are in trouble. Manhood, once an opportunity for achievement, now seems like a problem to be overcome. Plato, St. Francis, Leonardo daVinci, Vince Lombardi—you don't find guys of that caliber anymore. What you find is terrible gender anxiety. Guys trying to be Mr. Right. The man who can bake a cherry pie, go shoot skeet, come back and toss a salad, converse easily about intimate matters, cry if need be, laugh, hug, be vulnerable, perform passionately that night, and the next day go off and lift them bells onto that barge and tote it. Being perfect is a terrible way to spend your life. And guys are not equipped for it anyway. It's like a bear riding a bicycle, he can be trained to do it for short periods, but he would rather be in the woods doing what bears do there. - **An excerpt from Tender Warrior, by Stu Webber**

The point is well made. Men in our society today are very confused about who they are, and how they are supposed to act. What role are they supposed to play? It's the same for women. Their natural instincts of mothering and nurturing a family are constantly challenged by the liberal, feminist propaganda that says being a mom is a second-class role. So men and women are both searching for an identity with which they are comfortable.

When you don't have that core identity, and you cannot say with confidence, *"this is who I am, these are my values, this is my frame of reference, and this is my purpose,"* then you become what Zig Ziglar called a *"wondering generality, instead of a meaningful specific."*

We all need a strong foundation in our lives, so that no matter what happens around us, whether it is right or wrong, we will know who we are and how we ought to respond. You may have heard people say, "*the money changed him, or the loss of the business completely devastated him.*"

Well, if money can change someone for the worst, don't be fooled, they didn't know who they were in the first place. Or if the loss of a business devastates a person, then their identity was tied to the wrong thing.

When you have a strong identity base, you can always start over, regardless of what happens to you. When you know where you came from and who helped you get where you are, things like money don't change you for the worst. A strong sense of identity will give you confidence in every circumstance. You will have an air of certainty that causes people to notice and respect.

For Good or Bad

A strong sense of identity is not a respecter of persons. There is power in a strong identity, regardless of the person's core beliefs, whether good or bad. We can see from history how a person can hold beliefs that are considered evil by most people's standards, but because of their powerful personalities and confidence, people followed them. Men like Adolph Hitler and Jim Jones are examples of how evil men managed to get people to follow them simply because they had a strong and confident identity. Yes, it was a *bad* identity and a horribly destructive cause for which these men lived, but the power of their personal identity is seen in the outcome of their lives. They are not heroes by any stretch of the imagination, but the point is simple—a strong identity is powerful, for good or for bad.

The opposite is true as well. Many people have good intentions, but because they lack a strong identity they live ineffective and frustrating lives. They lack the power to make a difference for good in the world, simply because they do not have a strong core identity.

As you consider the power of personal identity, think for a moment about how your opinion of others affects the way you interpret their actions. For instance, if you have a favorable opinion of someone, you will typically interpret their actions in a good way; while the same actions taken by someone you mistrust will be viewed through a negative lens instead. If that is true about how you view the actions of others, does it not make sense that how you identify yourself is also going to affect how you view your own actions?

First, let's think about how you view others. Let's say you have a good friend named Gary and you think he is a good guy. He's a wonderful friend and an all around nice person. One day you see Gary and he is rude to you and behaves harshly towards you. Your first thought is that something is seriously wrong and Gary must be having a very bad day because it is so "out of character" for him to behave in such a way (or said another way, his actions are not within your defined identity for Gary). You do not react by thinking he is a jerk, because your identity of Jim has already pre-framed the way you interpret his actions. Your thoughts about the way he is acting causes you to pray for him and want to see how you could help him.

Now, let's totally change your identity of Gary. Let's say that based on your experiences with him in the past, you do not consider him to be a friend. He's actually someone you think would do anything for money. You don't trust him. You believe he has no integrity. Let's change his actions as well. Instead of him coming in and treating you harshly, he does just the opposite. He comes in and is *extra* nice to you. The first question that pops into your head is *"what does he want?"* As in the previous example, his current actions are not as important as the identity you already have of him. What you think of him controls how you interpret his behavior.

What influenced you the most about Gary in these two scenarios? Was it what he did, or your identity of him that mattered most?

Obviously, it was what you thought of him. Your identity of Gary had the greatest influence on your interpretation of what he did.

Identity is extremely powerful. If your opinion of Gary can affect how you interpret his actions, your opinion of yourself can also affect your interpretation of your own actions.

You Choose the Meaning

For instance, let's say you stop for gas and while the truck (I'm a Texas boy!) is filling up, you run in to the convenience store to get yourself something to drink. When you open the drink, it spills all over the place. How do you react? If you have a negative identity of yourself and think you are clumsy and always messing things up, then your reaction is going to be something like, "*I am always such a klutz.*"

If you have a confident identity your reaction will be different. You might say something like, "*somebody must have shaken this up.*" You are not going to immediately conclude that this happened because you are a klutz. I know that is a silly example, but the point is clear. How you see yourself affects not just the big stuff in life, it affects the little stuff as well.

When I am coaching my boys in baseball, I always remind them that what they say to themselves and the meaning they give to the events that happen on the field is important. For instance, if they miss a ground ball that came right to them when playing second base and immediately start thinking things like, "*I'm not a good ballplayer,*" or "*I always mess up,*" then they are in trouble. That kind of thinking affects their identity, and gives the wrong meaning to the incident.

On the other hand, they can have an identity of themselves that they are becoming great ballplayers because they work hard and improve every time they step on the field. Then, when they miss a ground ball, instead of having a perception that they are terrible, they will see it as a learning experience and think empowering thoughts such as, *"I didn't slide far enough, but I will next time,"* or *" I didn't have my glove down far enough, but I'm learning."* It's now a small mistake that they are going to learn from, instead of a defeating blow.

In life, as in baseball, what you say to yourself, and the personal identity you create for yourself, has a huge impact on the way you live your life. I've known people who have won great victories in their lives, yet because they don't see themselves as winners, they downplay the victory. They call it luck or a surprise blessing and cheat themselves out of seeing it as the victory that it is. I know God does give us surprise blessings, but don't rob yourself of the victories He also gives. Use those victories as opportunities to reinforce your identity as an overcomer, a winner, and a talented child of God.

People who have an awesome, unstoppable and empowered identity will experience something that most people would consider a failure, yet they turn it into a win. People with that kind of winning identity take failures and totally redefine them. The event becomes an awesome learning experience and a great opportunity to make a distinction.

Just like the kid who missed the ground ball. Instead of the "error" being something that reinforces a negative image, it becomes a learning experience. A chance to see exactly what he did wrong, and learn how to be an even better ballplayer after learning from that mistake.

Think of major league baseball players. Some might say that a person who "fails" to get a hit seven out of every ten at bats is a "failure." Meanwhile, that "failure" is probably making about Ten Million Dollars per year, because hitting .300 in the Majors will get you a healthy paycheck. Three out of every ten at bats, they get a hit and they get their confident identity from those three victories, not the seven "failures."

Just imagine how long a player would last if they ever let the "failures" at the plate reinforce an image of themselves as a lousy hitter. When they start thinking like that, those three out of ten hits start disappearing quickly (as does the paycheck). The players with amazing careers always manage to control the meaning they give to every experience at the plate and that makes all the difference. A strikeout or pop out is a learning experience and does not change their personal identity. They still see themselves as a great hitter with a rare gift. Even if they find themselves in a "slump," they keep telling themselves they have the ability and will work out of the slump. If they ever change their identity and start thinking, "Maybe I've lost it," then it's over for them!

Outcomes change depending upon how the outcome is defined in your own mind. How you respond to what happens to you is the most important thing. That response comes back to your identity of yourself.

How do you see yourself? Your personal identity influences every area of your life. If you want to live your purpose, it is vitally important that you develop a positive identity—a winner's identity. You've got to have an identity of yourself as someone who has a purpose and is working towards fulfilling specific plans and goals in your life.

So, let's begin with where you are right now. What is your current identity? As you answer the following questions in the workbook section, don't try to think too much about your answers. Write down whatever comes to mind. Remember, this is just a beginning.

1. How do you currently define yourself?

2. Who are you at your very core?

3. What do you believe?

4. What makes you different from others?

5. What are your skills?

6. What is your identity?

7. Why? What were the causes that created this particular identity of yourself?

3

DEVELOPING YOUR IDENTITY

Were you surprised by any of your answers to the questions in the previous chapter? Do you like how you see yourself? If not, don't worry. You're not stuck with yourself! If I was stuck with how I saw myself in high school I'd still be wearing a mullet and parachute pants, and I certainly wouldn't have written this book. I'm sure you can say the same thing (except hopefully not the part about parachute pants!).

The good news is we can always change and improve our identities. Zig Ziglar always said, "*yesterday ended last night, today is the first day of the rest of your life.*" Amen! Zig nailed it.

If you don't like the cards that life has dealt you, then get a new deck. You are the only one who has the power to do the changing.

Here's the most important thing to remember— whether you like the identity you have of yourself today or not, it is imperative that you actively create and reinforce your identity.

If you do not consciously engage in the development of your identity, then the influence of others, the circumstances that come into your life, and your own past experiences will take over and become the controlling factors.

Too often people allow their identities to be formed without thinking about it. I'm guessing that as you worked through the questions in the previous chapter, you saw that same thing in your own life. Many of your answers probably came from past experiences, the things people said to you, or your interpretation of events you went through. When those are the only determining factors forming your identity, you are no longer in control.

To begin changing the way you view yourself, you must actively participate in how your identity is being developed. If you allow outside influences to dictate what you think of yourself, then your identity will be beyond your control. As we saw in Chapter One, if you take responsibility for the way you respond to life and its challenges, you actually gain control.

If all of your life you were told that you were a looser and a klutz, sooner or later you would begin identifying yourself in that way. That identity, which was given to you by someone else, would become a part of who you are today, and in turn, would begin manifesting itself in all you do and say.

Circumstances can also control how our identities are formed. When things happen and you view them in a negative way, that meaning can become a part of your identity, and shape the way you live.

Big Moments

For instance, maybe you were the one who dropped that game winning catch when you were in high school. It was the final play of the game and the ball was coming right to you. Everyone was counting on you at that moment, and you blew it. Since then, you've always thought of yourself as someone who chokes under pressure. That identity has manifested itself in your life through your actions and decisions. You always avoid being in key roles because you believe that you will disappoint in clutch situations. It's become part of who you are—your identity.

If you allow the negative things that happen to you to form your identity, you will never fulfill your purpose. However, you can develop a new identity by identifying and changing the meaning of those negative events. Did missing that ball really mean that you could never be counted on again?

No, of course not!

It was just a bad day, everyone has them, but by allowing it to become a part of your identity it has affected the rest of your life.

The baseball version of this happened to me in my very last High School baseball game. I was the starting second baseman and lead off hitter. One of only three seniors, I felt a certain burden to lead and perform. We were in the playoffs against our archrival, those evil Coppell Cowboys.

Well, they weren't *really* evil, but we were the poor school out in the country and they were the rich kids from the other side of the tracks and it was High School, so I saw them as the bad guys!

It was the bottom of the final inning, one out, bases were loaded and I was on deck. Our nine-hole hitter was at the plate. I said to myself, "He's going to strike out, then I'm going to get a two-out, walk off hit and we're going to win this thing."

He struck out just as I thought and then the pitcher and I dueled into a full count. It was my dream situation. Last pitch of the game and bases loaded. If I get a hit, we win. If I walk, we tie it up and keep going. If I get out, game over and we lose.

The pitcher threw my favorite pitch, a fastball just a little high and right down the middle. In a millisecond, my mind knew it was going to be a solid hit right over the second baseman and we were going to win.

But I misjudged the pitch by a fraction, contacted the ball too low and popped out in shallow right field. I watched the ball easily fall into the right fielder's glove as I was running past first base with the full realization that my days of playing baseball ended in that moment.

My identity for the rest of my life would be greatly influenced, not by the event itself, but the meaning I gave the event. Fortunately, my father knew exactly what was at stake, and his words after the game framed things carefully and saved my identity from serious damage.

He could have said what many fathers say in that moment. *"You blew it. That was your chance. You could have been the hero, but you choked in the clutch situation. You will never live this down. I sure hope no lives are at stake next time you are expected to come through in the clutch, because you just can't handle the pressure."* Out of their own personal pride, wanting their son or daughter to be the hero so they can brag to their friends, they do real damage to the identity of the very person they love so much.

I've even caught myself crossing the line when wanting to encourage my kids to do their best and saying things (nothing like the above, but discouraging nonetheless) that were not best for developing their identity in a powerful way.

Not so with my father. His response after the game was not what one would normally expect. *"Wow, what an amazing baseball career. You came in as a freshman with virtually no baseball experience at all, ended up on varsity your first year, started the next three years, went to the playoffs all four years, the state finals your junior year, and then had an amazing senior year helping to lead your team to the playoffs. I'm so proud of you, son, and so glad I got to watch you play the game I love."*

My dad was an amazing baseball player, recruited by the St. Louis Cardinals when he was only sixteen, but he is an even more amazing father. His wisdom in carefully framing that moment for me would impact my identity for decades to come. What could have been a very negative defining moment became a blip on the screen of my life, and insignificant when stacked up against all the positive moments.

Have you had moments in your life that significantly impacted your identity in a negative way? Would you like to counter the negative influence of that moment?

Despite what has happened to you in the past, you can change your identity. It will be challenging, yes, but not impossible. The three main obstacles are:

1. Control – If you've always allowed other people or past events to create your identity for you, taking control will be a challenge. But the fact that you are reading this book tells me that you are up to the challenge!

2. Renewing your Mind – Changing your identity will mean changing the way you think and that may feel uncomfortable at first, even though it's old software that desperately needs to be updated.

3. Resistance to Change – It is natural to want to stay consistent with your identity. The known always seems better than the unknown. You must fight the desire to resist creating a new identity for yourself.

I've Heard it Both Ways

Identity is one of the strongest forces in the human personality. On the good side, this means that once you develop a healthy, powerful identity, it is hard to erode, no matter what happens. But that also means that it is going to take a lot of effort to transform a disempowering identity into an empowering one.

Your identity is like a thermostat for your life. If you set the thermostat in your home to 72 degrees, when the temperature in the house drops to 71 degrees the heater is going to kick in, and when it raises to 73 the air conditioner will come on. The thermostat ensures that the house is always at the same temperature.

In a similar fashion, your identity sets the temperature of your life. Let's say you have an identity of yourself as a 72-degree person. If your life starts dropping below the set mark of 72-degrees and you are living at 65 degrees instead, you begin making changes to get your life back on track. You know when you are living below the mark, because your life no longer reflects who you are. Whether it is your finances, relationships, spiritual or physical walk, whatever area of your life that has caused you to drop below your normal standard, you will do whatever it takes to get back to where you belong.

Now, let's say you really kick in the afterburners, and before you know it, you are living way above the level of where your identity says you should be living. You think you are a 72-degree person, but because you have been working so hard you are now living at the 95-degree level. All of a sudden, your subconscious mind takes over and you start slacking off and sabotaging your success until your life gets back down to that 72 degree mark where your identity of yourself says that you deserve to be.

Most of the time, you do not even realize it is happening. People sabotage themselves in order to bring themselves down to the level where they really think they ought to be living, simply because that is how they identify themselves.

My own father sabotaged his business success several times. I remember him explaining to me that in his own mind, he felt like he did not deserve all the success he was experiencing. He had grown up dirt poor in what we affectionately call "the sticks." His family didn't even have running water until later in his life. The level of success that he rose to was absolutely unbelievable. By the age of 26, my father had made enough money to retire. Can you imagine that?

He was incredibly successful, yet he felt like he didn't deserve that kind of success because he still had the identity of a poor country boy who had wondered far from home. Subconsciously he felt out of place. He wasn't aware that he was thinking this way, but he started sabotaging his success and losing what he had gained as he subconsciously tried to get back to what he thought was 72 degrees for his life.

So, no matter how badly you want something, whether it is success, strong relationships, a purpose filled life, or to reach a particular goal, if you do not adjust and modify your core identity along the way, you might sabotage yourself instead.

To have the right identity you need to be constantly renewing your mind. Just as the Bible teaches us in Romans 12:2,

> *Be transformed by the renewing of your mind,*
> *that you may prove what is that good and*
> *acceptable and perfect will of God.*

If you don't do that then you can implement everything else in this program, experience wild success, and still destroy it all because you didn't have the right identity from the beginning.

Developing your identity is a continual life-long process.

One day, all could be going well, with you making progress on living your purpose, and the thermostat at just the right level. Then something completely outside your control happens, and before you know it, the temperature suddenly drops to 65 degrees. You will, Lord Willing, work hard to get things back up to the degree you desire. We all have those days (sometimes entire seasons!).

The danger comes when success does not come as quickly as desired. Many give up at that point and get comfortable living at 65 degrees. Instead of pressing on and getting back to the desired "temperature," they give up and reset the thermostat. They lower their standards. It happens to people all the time. They decide it's not worth the fight, or they stop believing things will get better, so they decide to live at the lower standard, missing out on their greatest purpose.

Has this happened in your career? Your marriage? Your relationship with God?

The good news is you don't have to fall into those traps. You can change your identity for the better. You can develop the characteristics and traits that you really want.

One way to change your identity is by simply talking to people who have traits in their lives that you admire. Ask them how they developed that trait and begin applying the same principles to your life. Implement the strategies that you admire in others. You will begin to see the same character traits develop in your life.

Is there a person or persons that you admire and would desire to be more like if you could? What would your life be like if you had some of the character traits that you admire most in that person.

Take a moment to think about that.

Really. I'm serious.

STOP READING for a moment and truly consider this.

Did you actually consider the possibilities or just keep reading?

I'm not suggesting that you indulge in flights of fancy, but rather that you would see the power of what is realistically possible in your life.

Imagine being the kind of person you would like to be. What would that look like for you? What would change? Would you be more vibrant, serious, generous, spiritual, or dedicated? What would your life look like if you could be who you want to be? How would that affect the way you treat those around you?

It's nice to think about the possibilities that exist.

The question is: *Are you going to live like that?*

It is possible. And it is going to take some effort on your part, as well as some help from mentors around you who have successfully gone before you. Before you can go out and be successful you must begin thinking of yourself in that way. You've got to work on your identity first, so that you are prepared for the success and the opportunities that God is going to bring to you.

As you answer the questions at the end of this chapter, you will be creating a full list of the character traits you would like to have. It will take an investment of your time to do this activity. Fill out the answers the best you can for now. Remember, this is a process. You don't have to turn this paperwork into anybody. It is not a test. Over the weeks, months, and years to come, you are going to come back and refine your answers as you build up your purpose and your life plan.

1. Describe the person you would like to be?

2. How would you like for people to describe you?

3. If your pastor or spouse or one of your children were telling someone about you, what would you want to be said?

4. How do you want to be remembered?

5. Before making a list of character traits you would like to exhibit in your life, answer the following questions:

a.   Describe your favorite Bible hero.

b.   Describe the ideal employer or business partner. If you could pick the perfect person to work for or with what characteristics would they have?

c.   The perfect employee? What would they be like if you could design them yourself?

d.   What characteristics would you give to the absolutely perfect mate? What are the characteristics you see in your mate that you really love, admire, respect, and enjoy? What are the characteristics you would like for them to have that they don't exemplify all the time?

e.   Think of someone you really admire and respect— what character traits would you use to describe him or her?

From your answers above, make a list below of the character traits that you would like to see exhibited in your life.

4

RENEWING YOUR MIND

Congratulations!

That last chapter was a lot of work. But if you put your heart and soul into it, you should now have a pretty good picture of the identity you would like to have. Knowing what you would like to engrain into yourself is an essential step in beginning to live your purpose.

Now that you have a list of the character traits that you want to develop as part of your identity, I encourage you to begin doing something that Zig Ziglar taught me to do a long time ago.

Handwrite each of those character traits on the center of a 3x5 index card. Do your best to sum up each trait into one word (i.e. courageous, faithful, etc.). Every morning as you are getting ready for the day, stand in front of the mirror and read those character traits to yourself like this, *"I am courageous... I am faithful..."* and continue until you read each card.

You will be building and reinforcing your identity as it becomes a reality in your life.

Have some fun with this! Read the cards with conviction—say it like you mean it. If you are embarrassed, remember that you are the only one looking into that mirror. Why would you be embarrassed?

It's just you!

If you want to take it to the next level and do one of the most effective things you can with this exercise, ask your spouse if they would be willing to read your cards to you. Perhaps you are both creating your life plan at the same time. GREAT! You can also read theirs to them.

Imagine how powerful it will be to have the most important person in your life telling you that you are *courageous, faithful* and whatever other traits you have listed on your cards.

In this way, you are acting out Ephesians 4:22-24, by training yourself to put off the old and put on the new, which was created according to God.

Put off, concerning your former conduct, the old man which grows corrupt according to the deceitful lusts, and be renewed in the spirit of your mind, and that you put on the new man which was created according to God, in true righteousness and holiness.

As you work on developing your identity and living your purpose, keep a few things about human nature in mind.

Oh, Be Careful Little Tongue What You Say

First, I would encourage you not to get into the habit of condemning things that you want when you see them in other people. When you see someone who is enjoying something that you would like to enjoy one day, resist the temptation to condemn it out of jealousy. Don't say things like, "*he only got that because his daddy got him the job*" or, "*she only got that because she went into massive debt.*"

I remember a time when I would verbally shoot down other speakers because they were enjoying the kind of success that I wanted. I'd mumble about why I should be on stage instead of them. But in truth—I was jealous. They were doing exactly what I wanted to do, and I was condemning them because I was seeing it in their life, instead of my own.

Then one day, I realized that I was setting myself up for failure by making accusations against the successes of others. I learned that the more I condemned their accomplishments, the more I was creating bad associations in my own heart and mind for the things I wanted to achieve. In a sense, I was working against myself. Every time I criticized another speaker, I was subconsciously telling myself that I didn't want what they had, when in fact I really did.

I finally stopped making accusations against others and started blessing them instead. I thanked the Lord for how He was using that person and for giving me such a wonderful role model to follow. I began to believe that if they could do it, I could do it as well and that encouraged me to keep working towards my goals.

When you see one of your dreams being fulfilled in someone else's life, regardless of who they are or how you think they managed to do it, say to yourself, *"if they can do it, I can do it."* And thank God for giving you an example in them.

Second, follow Paul's admonition in Ephesians 4:29:

Let no corrupt communication proceed out of your mouth, but what is good for necessary edification, that it may impart grace to the hearers.

In this case, I believe that the hearers include us. Whenever we speak negatively about others or ourselves, we are not edifying. We are tearing down.

If you are continually saying to yourself, *"I can't believe I just did that...I'm such an idiot...I always mess things up...Things never work out for me.... etc.,"* that will negatively reinforce the way you think about yourself—your identity.

My dad engrained this in me as a child. He would always correct me whenever he heard me saying anything negative about myself. He would tell me that I was going to start believing what I was saying, and eventually I would end up living it out. He was absolutely right.

You need to do the same. As soon as you catch yourself saying negative statements such as *"nothing every works out for me."* Stop! Replace it with an empowering statement that reverses that thought.

Start reminding yourself that the Bible says just the opposite. It says *"ALL things work together for good for those who love the Lord and are called according to His purposes."* So if you love the Lord and are working on living with purpose, then all things are working together for good for you, even when it doesn't feel that way.

If you find yourself saying something like, *"I'm so big and fat…"* Stop, and remind yourself of the truth. You are the temple of the Living God and out of respect for Him and for yourself you are working on creating a healthy, appealing body.

Of course, you have to be practical about it as well. You cannot expect to *affirm* the fat away while scarfing down the donuts and ice cream. You've got to take the necessary actions. You have to *say* the right things as well as *do* the right things. These are two extremely powerful building blocks in your life.

High Quality Building Materials for the Brain

A wise builder uses only the best materials. You would not hire a builder to build your family home if he was going to use rotten wood, crooked beams, old carpets, or rusty pipes. You would want a home that was built with all the best materials so that it would last a lifetime and keep your family safe.

Certainly, if you would be that careful about what goes into building your home, you should be even more diligent to use only the best materials when forming your thoughts and identity. The old saying, *"garbage in, garbage out"* is absolutely true when it comes to what you allow to enter into your mind.

So much "mind trash" is out there today. You and I need to stand guard at the gate of our minds and be careful what we allow to come inside. It's not just a matter of positive thinking, it so much more! The fact is your mind is a battlefield. Whatever you allow to influence you the most will win your thoughts, and that will impact your outcome.

That influence comes in many forms, such as music, movies, television, what you read, and the people you associate with each day. Anyone who thinks they can listen to trash, watch trash, read trash, and hang out with trash, and then not live out trash is absolutely delusional.

I am not suggesting we all go live in a commune on a mountaintop, but I am saying you should control what you are allowing to influence you, as best you can. Every time you allow negative and disrespectful music or programs into your mind, you are programming your brain to exhibit those things in your life.

From Mickey Mouse to Bart Simpson

Anyone who has raised children knows the influence that television can have on their lives. Not all of it is bad; however, too much of the programming that is aimed at children (even on the Disney Channel) is filled with teenagers who have smart mouths, lousy work ethic, and disrespectful attitudes towards their parents.

A few years ago, Kara and I noticed our children picking up and reflecting some of the bad attitudes from some of the shows they were watching on the Disney channel, so we shut it off. We got tired of our children acting like all those disrespectful kids on those shows.

All of us must recognize that what comes in, is going to come out.

Once, I heard Zig Ziglar talking about a cultural survey that was done to see what the number one selling t-shirts were in certain countries. In Japan at the time, it was *We're Number One.* Can you imagine the positive impact that would have on the person wearing it, and on society in general?

In America, unfortunately, it was the cartoon character, Bart Simpson saying, *Underachiever and Proud of It.*

There is not an ounce of positive impact from that t-shirt.

In fact, I cannot think of a more negative impacting television program on a generation than *The Simpsons.* I remember in college, it seemed as though that show was always on in the recreation room.

In those formidable teen and early adult years, my generation was constantly being bombarded with programing that promoted a ridiculous, vulgar, underachiever and proud of it mentality, and unfortunately for many, it became part of their identities. In fact, it has had a massively negative impact on the work ethic of the entire X and Y generations. As a group, we are lazier and more reliant on government programs than any previous generation.

The only way we are going to turn around the affects of such a negative onslaught on the minds of a generation is to do it one person at a time. When individuals are determined not to allow those kinds of influences to enter into their brains any longer, they can make a difference on the rest of the world around them.

> *Finally, brethren, whatever things are true, whatever things are noble, whatever things are just, whatever things are pure, whatever things are lovely, whatever things are of good report, if there is any virtue and if there is anything praiseworthy— meditate on these things.* - **Philippians 4:8**

When you start thinking about those things, it turns your mind around and gives you the right perspective on what you need to be doing in the culture, community, family, and even in the nation.

A pastor friend of mine, John Melvin, once said from the pulpit,

> *If you take a glass full of oil—nasty, dirty oil—right out of an engine that hadn't been changed for 5,000 miles, and put it in the sink and run pure water into that glass for a while, eventually it will push out the oil. At first it will be kind of murky, then it will start to change from being jet black to being dark brown, then light brown, but it will still be oily. But if you let that water, pure water, (like good thoughts, positive elements) run into that glass long enough eventually the water in the glass will be as pure as bottled water.*

That is exactly how our brains work too. Whatever you watch, listen to, and concentrate on, is going to influence your mind. It is going to create your thoughts, and your thoughts will in turn create your reality. So, stand guard at the gate of your mind, and at the minds of your children. Our generation is depending on it. The future of this country is depending on it.

1.   Have you ever condemned the very things you want? Who are some people in whom you have seen the things you want; yet you spoke negatively about them in some way? Write down what your statement could be in the future when you see

the things you want in other people. (Example: God Bless him for being such a great leader, I'm glad to have a good role model.)

2.   What are some negative statements you have made about yourself that you are willing to commit to never saying again?

3.   What are some encouraging statements you could use to replace those negative statements?

4.   What are some negative ingredients you have mixed into your identity that you are willing to remove? (Examples: certain music, entertainment, etc.)

BELIEFS

5

YOUR BELIEF SYSTEM

Beliefs are incredibly powerful. What you believe has a tremendous impact on the way you live.

Dr. Bernie Siegle of Yale University did a lot of research on this subject. He studied people who were known to have multiple personality disorders. These subjects suffered from a mental illness that caused them to change personalities and totally believe they were a completely different person. He found their belief systems were so powerful, they actually experienced changes in their biochemistry when they switched personalities. By believing they were a totally different person, sometimes their bodies would actually transform right in front of the researchers. I don't mean they grew an extra arm, but their eye color would literally change. Physical marks would disappear and reappear. Diseases, such as diabetes or high blood pressure would come and go depending upon which personality they were experiencing.

A New Drug for Huey Lewis & The News

Another example of how powerful our belief systems can be is seen in psychological studies where patients were given placebo pills, which are nothing more than a sugar pill, but told that they were taking drugs that would cure their ailments and in many instances the cure would result. In these cases, the patient's belief that the pill would cure them was more powerful than their current physical condition.

Beliefs can even overpower drugs. Not only can they be like a drug, they can override a drug's affect to the point of even obtaining opposite results. In a study conducted by Dr. Henry Beecher of Harvard University, some students were given a super stimulant and told it was a super tranquilizer. While other students were given a super tranquilizer and told it was a super stimulant. Half of all the students got the results they were told the drug was supposed to give—that means they experienced exactly the opposite results than the drug normally created, because that is what they believed would happen. Their beliefs literally reversed the effect of the drug in their bodies.

That's remarkable. We're not talking about a sugar pill or the mind playing tricks on the body. This is the mind overcoming the effects of an actual drug that is working its chemistry within the body. Beliefs are incredibly powerful.

Have you ever known someone who took an aspirin and almost immediately said that they felt better? Most pain relievers typically take a minimum of fifteen minutes to work, and could take up to an hour. Yet, oftentimes people feel better much quicker. Why? Because they believe that the drug they just took will take away their pain. It probably will in fifteen minutes, but if they feel better immediately then it is the belief itself that is giving them relief from their pain.

Beliefs play a vital role not only in the way they affect your physical body, but also in how they influence everything you do. What you believe influences whether or not you will discover and fulfill your purpose. Therefore, pay close attention to your belief system. Take time to consider whether a belief might have been created for you by other people, or by circumstances in your life, without any actual analysis on your part.

First, let's take a look at what I mean by your belief system. Your belief system is much more than just what you believe, spiritually. Yes, this is an important part of your belief system, but it is not the only aspect. Your belief system encompasses much more—it is the sum and total of what you believe about yourself, your abilities, your calling, and your purpose in life.

Belief systems separate those who *want* to make a difference from those who actually do.

Whether You Think You Can or Think You Can't, You're Right!

As discussed in the previous section on *identity*, we see this a lot in sports. As a coach for my boys' baseball team, I would often see a kid who had great natural talent but who performed poorly during games because he did not believe he could play well. On the other hand, I would see players who did not have even half of the same natural talent or ability, but they performed better on the field because they believed they could get the hits and make the plays.

That is something that occurs even amongst the professional athletes. Now obviously, a professional athlete has to have a certain amount of natural talent, size, and ability. But there are many players who have all those things, yet they have never made it big. Only one out of ten minor league professional players make it to the major leagues. The difference between those who make it to "the show" and those who never break through often boils down to their personal belief systems.

Football also provides a number of great examples of the power of a person's belief system. In 1957, there was a ten-year-old boy who started setting goals for his life. He wanted to be like his hero, Jim Brown, who was the greatest running back ever, at that time. To most of the people who knew the boy, his goal seemed impossible. Growing up in the ghetto, malnutrition had taken its toll on him. He had rickets that forced him to wear steal splints to support his skinny and bowed legs. He couldn't even afford to buy a ticket to the game. But he would wait patiently outside the players gate, hoping to get Jim Brown's autograph as he was leaving the field.

One day, he had his chance to ask Jim Brown for his autograph and as Brown was signing his name, the boy told him, *"Mr. Brown I have your picture on my wall, I know you hold all the records, you are my idol."* Brown smiled and began to leave, but the young boy hadn't finished. He said, "Mr. Brown, one day I'm going to break every record you hold." Brown was impressed, and he asked him his name. The boy replied, "Orenthal James, my friends call me OJ." OJ Simpson went on to break all but three of the rushing records held by Jim Brown before injuries shortened his football career.

Now, I know that OJ is not the best example to use, but I chose him in order to make an additional point. Strong belief systems are no respecter of persons.

Beliefs Control Your Perspective

Beliefs are so powerful that two people can experience the exact same event and come away with totally different perspectives. Each of their accounts of the event will be colored by their individual belief systems. It will affect the meaning, interpretation, and perspective of the event. Recall from the previous chapters on *identity*, what you believe about an event will determine how that event will ultimately affect your life.

For instance, there were two men who were shot down in Vietnam and taken to a POW camp. For the seven years they were in that place, they both endured the same treatment: isolation, frequent beatings, rusted shackles, and constant torture, but they came out of it with very different perspectives. One man tragically committed suicide. The other says he would not trade those seven years for any other experience. His name is Captain Gerald Coffey. Captain Coffey turned that nightmare into an opportunity to draw closer to the Lord and that is what sustained and strengthened him through that experience.

Captain Coffey is a living example of the power of a belief system. He was not only able to endure because of what he believed, but he was able to come away with a positive outcome from a devastating ordeal. My wife, Kara, and I had the opportunity to have dinner with Captain Coffey and his wife a few years ago when I was speaking in Hawaii. The fact that he could go through all he did, and then allow God to use his experience to make him a stronger and better man is an inspiring story for all of us.

We see the power of belief systems at work in the business world as well. Many have become multi-millionaires after bankruptcy, while others have committed suicide, or simply given up on their dreams, after experiencing a bankruptcy. What causes the difference? It is their belief systems.

People like Walt Disney, Henry Ford, and even my own father experienced bankruptcy, but went on to have great success.

I believe even our health and longevity can be influenced by our belief systems. My great-grandfather lived to be One Hundred and One years old. One of his jobs had been literally digging graves for other people until he was about eighty-eight years old. He continued to live life for all it was worth until his body finally gave out.

Many believe retirement at sixty-five means retiring from life. They sit down and wait to die and that belief system takes root. What was it that made my great-grandfather different? He would have told you it was his Red Man Chewing Tobacco, but I'm pretty sure that what made him different was his belief system.

Different Beliefs = Different Results

In the Old Testament, Moses sent twelve men to spy out the Promised Land. They all saw the same thing, giants, incredible fruit, and milk and honey. Ten of them came back saying it was impossible to enter into the land. They saw the challenges before them and believed there was no way they could succeed. They whined and cried and persuaded the people that there was no way they can do it. They depressed an entire generation and that generation died in the wilderness due to their negative report. That was the result of their negative thinking and limiting beliefs.

Joshua and Caleb were also among the secret agents that Moses sent into the land. They saw the same giants, amazing fruit, and the milk and honey. Their response was completely the opposite of the other spies. They encouraged the people to enter into the land. They were convinced they could win because they believed that God had given them the land. They tried to convince the people to enter in and take the land, but the negative belief systems of the people caused them to side with the ten spies that had "stinkin' thinkin'" (a Zigism) and refused to go.

The people allowed the limiting beliefs of the other ten to affect their decision and they missed out on the greatest blessing of their lives. They missed out on their calling and their purpose, so it had to be passed to the next generation. Take a moment to ponder the implication of that statement. God had a calling and a purpose for them, but their belief systems and their responses caused them to completely miss their highest calling and purpose.

Are you missing out on your highest calling and purpose because of limiting beliefs? Stick that one in your pipe and smoke on it, we will come back to it later.

Why was there such a difference of opinion among the spies over the exact same set of circumstances? All twelve spies saw the same thing, but only two of them, Joshua and Caleb, had empowering beliefs—they believed they could enter into the land. The other ten had limiting beliefs—they thought it was impossible to enter into the land.

In each of the examples we see that it is not the events that happened, but the responses to what happened that made the difference. The event does not determine the outcome. What you *believe* about the event is going to determine the impact it has on your life.

Joshua and Caleb believed that God would do what He said He would do and this influenced their reaction to what they saw in the Promised Land. The other ten men just kept thinking about the giants, while Joshua and Caleb saw all the benefits that God had promised as their reward. They were willing to go fight. They knew it would not happen overnight. They knew it was going to be hard work. They knew it was going to be incremental, but they were willing to go because of their belief system.

What is your belief system? It will determine the meaning you give to every event that happens in your life.

If you believe that at seventy-years of age your body is worn out and you are about to die, then when you turn seventy and maybe even before, you are going to start acting and believing that you are about to die. You are going to bring about your own self-fulfilling prophecy.

If, on the other hand, you adopt a belief system that says, "Age seventy equals wisdom and freedom," you are going to have a much better chance of being like my great grandfather. You are going to live every day for all it is worth regardless of your age. You are going to make the most of the wisdom that you've gathered over those seventy years and find ways to pass that on to the next generation. You will continue to invest in freedom and do things that will make a difference to the people around you.

If you are young and have a belief system that says you must have grey hair and at least ten years experience before you can start your own successful business, how is that going to affect your outcome? It will cause you to miss opportunities. It will cause you not to be bold. It will cause you not to take the risk. You certainly will not attempt to be an entrepreneur until you are older. You will not decide to venture out. Those beliefs are going to cause you to self-sabotage, or essentially enter hibernation mode until the "acceptable" age is reached. Remember what it says in Mark 9:23, *all things are possible to him who believes*. What you allow yourself to believe will either hold you back from greatness, or catapult you towards it.

The One-Minute Mile

Prior to April 1954, it was believed and widely accepted that it was physically impossible for a man to run a mile in less than four minutes. Since the days of the early Greeks, there were people attempting to break the mark, but it had never been done. Doctors said it was impossible for the body to perform such a feat.

But one man believed differently.

He trained in a way that reflected and represented his beliefs. Those who had attempted in the past were also in top physical shape, but there was something different about this man. He had the top physical shape *and* he had the right belief system.

Roger Bannister trained his mind to see the event before it even took place. He played the mental movie of breaking the mark. He trained his body and his brain and in April 1954, he shocked the sports world by running the mile in less than four minutes. That was pretty impressive, but only the beginning.

The amazing part of the story is what happened next. Within a year, dozens of people had done the same thing. Within two years, hundreds of people had broken the mark, and to this day, tens of thousands have done it.

Yet, prior to Bannister, no one in the history of the world had run at that speed. What do you think changed?

Gravity?

Do you think Nike Air tennis shoes maybe had something to do with it? No, they weren't even around yet.

It was the power of the belief structure. When the limiting belief was lifted, the body and the brain were able to fulfill their potential.

The answer to the question at the beginning of this section, *"what is it that separates those who want to make a difference from those who actually do?"* is belief.

Once a belief has been established in your brain, your nervous system responds. It can be very limiting to our future, if the belief is not an empowering one, because it causes us to shut down.

The opposite is also true. Empowering beliefs expand the possibilities. That is why it is so important to take an inventory of what you believe. Your beliefs will dictate your decisions, and in turn those decisions will dictate your destiny.

The belief system you have today was created gradually, over time, as you gave meaning to the events and experiences that came into your life.

This belief system now defines who you are and determines what you do.

When you study the lives of successful people, one of the most important character traits you find is that they give positive, empowering meanings to whatever happens to them, whether good or bad. When they make a conscious decision about what an event means, they tend to give it an empowering meaning instead of a disempowering one. They refuse beliefs that would limit them and reinforce those beliefs that will strengthen them.

Part of the goal of this book is to help you develop an ongoing system of analyzing your beliefs. This will enable you to see where they are coming from, and how they are affecting your decisions.

This is a continual process that you are beginning now, but you will work on as you plan and live your purpose in the months and years to come. As you come back and analyze what your belief systems are periodically, you will look for ways to get rid of the bad, limiting beliefs, and create new and empowering ones in their place.

Remember, beliefs can limit you or they can catapult you. The question is, "What are your beliefs?" Are they limiting your ability to pursue your purpose and live your life to the fullest?

Limiting beliefs are the reason that most people wake up dreading the day. They have allowed themselves to believe things will not get any better. They feel they can do nothing to change where they are in life.

My goal is to make sure you are not part of that crowd. I want to make sure that what you believe is not limiting you or holding you back, but is giving you the power to fulfill your purpose.

It's a Matter of Perspective

The first thing you need to do is to take an inventory of your current belief system. You are going to analyze the beliefs you hold right now and determine whether they are empowering ones, or limiting ones. Then you are going to look at how to get rid of the limiting beliefs you have and how to strengthen the empowering ones.

Before you begin working on the questions, let me give you an example from my own life. I started in business when I was twenty years old, while I was still in law school. I had a very limiting belief at that time that nagged at me. It was a belief that I was too young to be in business. I did not believe that I had any credibility because of my age, and that limiting belief caused me to self-sabotage many opportunities. It held me back, and kept me from being bold and stepping out in some of the things that I wanted to do at that time.

I could not change the circumstance. I could not make myself older in an instance. So I had to change my perspective regarding my youth. I had to replace the disempowering belief with an empowering one.

I began looking at my youth as something that was adding to my credibility instead of taking it away. The fact that I had the ability to lead at such a young age, and to accomplish the number of things I had in such a short period of time, was a credit, not a detriment.

By changing my perspective on the circumstance, I began to get different results. Instead of having a limiting belief because of my age, I was now empowered by it and it actually allowed me to move even faster towards the purpose in my life. Once I saw it as an empowering circumstance, it actually encouraged me to do more. I ran for office at the age of twenty-six.

Rather than avoiding the topic of my age, I talked about my youth as a positive, emphasizing how I had already had businesses and done things at a young age. That caused people to think of me as a go-getter and someone who could shake things up in the legislature. I won the election, but it would not have happened if I had not changed my limiting belief into an empowering one.

Now it's your turn. The first thing I'm going to ask you to do is take the time to look closely and identify your belief systems. Write them all down. Make a list of those beliefs that are helping you towards your purpose, and those that are hindering you or keeping you from living your purpose.

Your limiting beliefs may not be the same as mine. But no matter how big or small they may seem, I want you to write any limiting beliefs that you catch yourself buying into today, so you can replace them with empowering ones.

1. What are your limiting beliefs?

2. How are these limiting beliefs holding you back from living your purpose?

3. What will it cost you to keep these limiting beliefs?

4. What could you gain if you were to lose these limiting beliefs?

5. What are your empowering beliefs?

6. How are these empowering beliefs helping you to live your purpose?

7. What would you gain if you could strengthen these empowering beliefs?

You cannot change the events of your life, but you have total control over their meaning.

Ask better questions.

Instead of *"why me?"* how about *"what's your plan for me?"*

6

HOW BELIEFS ARE DEVELOPED

Now that you have identified some of the beliefs in your life, it is time to focus on getting rid of the limiting ideas, and reinforcing the empowering ones.

In this chapter, you are going to learn to do that by using pain and pleasure to produce change. By associating pain with your limiting beliefs and pleasure with your empowering ones, you will begin to get rid of those things that are hindering you, and strengthen those things that are helping you live your purpose.

You have already begun the process by answering the questions in the previous chapter that dealt with how your limiting beliefs were holding you back, and your empowering beliefs were moving you forward.

Knowing what you are gaining and losing as a result of your beliefs is a great motivation for making positive changes.

When you look at your list of limiting beliefs, remember the good news—you are not sentenced to a life of limiting beliefs! You don't have to keep any of them if you don't want to. The choice is yours.

Where Did That Idea Come From?

In order to be able to wipe out your limiting beliefs, it's important to understand exactly what a *belief* is and how it is established in your life. The best explanation I've heard compares a belief to a table. The tabletop is the idea and the legs underneath the tabletop are the references and experiences that support the idea, whether good or bad.

Take a moment to picture a tabletop with no legs underneath to support it. Essentially, it is a piece of wood lying on the floor. In this analogy, the tabletop is an idea.

A belief is a tabletop (idea) that has strong legs underneath, supporting it. Those legs represent the references, or experiences in your life that have strengthened certain ideas to the point where they have become strong beliefs and convictions.

For example, consider a young baseball player whose coach constantly berates him and tells him that he is no good. With each dropped ball and strike out, the player will soon begin to believe that he cannot play the game. The idea that he is no good, planted in his mind by the coach, is being strengthened by each negative experience on the field.

If you say to that same kid, *"you've got some raw talent, you've got a great swing, you just need to work on it."* You have now planted the idea that he has potential and every sign of improvement on the field will become the legs supporting and reinforcing the belief that he is a good player.

96

This is *not* about lavishing empty platitudes or positive reinforcement without the necessary instruction or ability that needs to go along with the words of encouragement.

You cannot just say to someone, "*you can do it, you can do it*" unless there is a realistic expectation that they can do it. Without showing them how or encouraging them to work harder to be their best, they will not be able to do it and you will have set them up for failure.

What I am talking about is inspiring others to believe that if they do the work necessary, they can realistically expect to get better. So, instead of striking out and going away defeated, that young baseball player will go home and hit the ball off the tee 200 times a day to develop his swing.

Your beliefs are created by the combination of experiences (legs) connected to ideas (the tabletop). Once you have enough strong legs supporting your ideas (whether they are good or bad), they become beliefs and convictions in your life. That is how beliefs become established.

In the past, you probably have allowed others to create your beliefs for you. Or, perhaps the circumstances of your life may have piled up under certain ideas, and beliefs were established. It happens quite naturally. That is why it is important to be aware of your belief system and continually work on getting rid of those limiting beliefs.

The beliefs you have depend upon the references in your life. For instance, based on different experiences you might say, "*I think all evangelists are charlatans. They are deceiving, lying, money hungry fakes.*" Or, you could say, "*I think evangelists are awesome. They are giving, humble, powerful human beings that make a difference.*" If the large majority of evangelists you have known have proven to be awesome people, those references are stronger and you have a good view of evangelists. On the other hand, if an evangelist or pastor or some other "Christian" took advantage of you, stole money, or did not do something they said they were going to do, and it was an intensely emotional experience, you may have a negative perception of evangelists.

In most cases, you will have a mix of experiences that could support several different conclusions. The determining factor becomes which experience you choose to focus on and give the most credibility. Whichever legs you choose will determine what your ultimate belief is going to be. You may have references that back up either belief in any situation. A baseball player has plenty of references that will say they are a lousy hitter and plenty of references that will say they are a great hitter. To which reference do they give the most attention?

If one of my players has two strikeouts, a home run and a triple, I am constantly reminding them after the game that they need to purposely focus in on the homerun and the triple and engrain it in their memory and remember those moments. That's the reference that gives strength to the belief that they can hit.

Some kids go home thinking about nothing but the strikeouts, even though they had great at bats their other times up. But all they can think about is the failure. That reinforces the belief that they are failures and that's why most kids do not make it to the next level in baseball. Very few of the folks that start playing baseball make it to the major leagues and this belief system is a huge part of it.

As mentioned earlier in the identity chapters, physical talent has a huge impact on it as well, but believe me there are a ton of ball players with all the physical talent that don't make it because of their belief system.

Now that you have a little understanding on how beliefs are formed in your life, it is time to get to work on getting rid of some of your limiting beliefs. You are going to get rid of cach supporting leg that has given you a limiting belief. At the same time, you are going to create plenty of legs that reinforce empowering beliefs instead.

Mental Inventory Management

You are going to start by taking an inventory of the legs, or reference points, for a limiting belief in your life. You may find that after rationally analyzing what you *thought* was evidence for the belief, you simply lose the belief after realizing that the references were nothing more than silly events that did not matter much.

On the other hand, you may find that your belief has some valid references that are strong and deserved and you might decide to keep it.

At the end of this chapter, you will take the list of beliefs you discovered in the last chapter and list all the references that strengthen that belief. If you have trouble thinking of the references, ask yourself what happened to make you adopt this belief. If you don't know, I understand. But if you do know, include all of those references. Every experience that gave you that belief should be listed.

You will then use carefully designed questions to help you accomplish three things:

- Use pain and pleasure to change the belief.
- Create doubt in the current belief.
- Create new legs and strengthen old legs that support an empowering belief to replace the limiting belief.

What is it worth to you to get rid of the limiting belief and replace it with an empowering belief that will allow you to live your life with purpose?

Go through each question and project yourself down the road five or ten years, dragging all of the pain that comes with that limiting belief. If there is enough negativity associated to the belief, you will want to get away from it. It's going to take some time but it is well worth it. It's going to be one of the best investments you've ever made. Take the time to answer each question, and don't forget that this is not a once in a lifetime activity. This is something you are going to do on an ongoing basis as you pick up new beliefs each day.

If they are limiting, we want to get rid of them. If they are empowering we want to enforce them.

If you are willing to adopt the belief that you can change and control your beliefs, it could be one of the most empowering activities you will ever do. Beliefs are powerful and you have to become flexible in controlling your beliefs if you want to multiply that power and allow yourself to live with purpose.

I love the words to that old song by Petra. It says: *You can pull down strongholds if you just believe you can.*

You can pull down strongholds. It works if you implement this process. Beliefs are powerful, but they can also be limiting. The choice is yours. What will you do today to live with purpose?

Ask yourself the following seven questions about each of your limiting beliefs.

1. **Was the person I gained the references from worth modeling, were they an expert, and was their "expertise" empowering to me?**

2. How will this belief negatively affect my relationships for the rest of my life and what will it ultimately cost me in the relationships area of my life if I don't get rid of the belief? (What will it cost my family?) Be very specific.

3. How will this belief negatively affect me spiritually, and what will it ultimately cost me in this area if I don't get rid of the belief?

4. How will this belief negatively affect me financially, and what will it ultimately cost me in the financial area of my life if I don't get rid of the belief?

5. How will this belief negatively affect me physically, and what will it ultimately cost me in the physical area of my life if I don't get rid of the belief?

6. How is this belief ridiculous or absurd?

7. What references do I have that could possibly NOT support this "belief?" What things do you know to be true that could reverse those references?

Now, let's link some extra pain to those disempowering beliefs and get rid of them for good:

1. Think of every single horrible thing that this limiting belief could cause in your life. Think specifically through each area of your life: your spiritual walk, your family, your friends, your career, your finances, your physical health, and even your legacy.

2. Project yourself five years into the future, dragging all that pain with you. What will you have missed out on because you didn't get rid of this limiting belief? What pain will your family have gone through? Where will you be in five years because of this belief?

3. Project yourself ten years into the future, dragging all that pain and ask yourself the same questions.

4. Go twenty years into the future and ask each and every question. Make it real. The more real and emotional you make it, the more pain you create and the more likely you will create

change.

5. Realize that none of that has happened yet and you have the chance to reverse it, to prevent it, and to cause the exact opposite.

6. Turn back to where you listed the limiting belief and it's references. Scratch out the limiting belief. Write down an empowering belief that would replace it. (For me, a limiting belief was that I was too young to be successful. I replaced it with "Youth is powerful!")

7. Associate massive pleasure to the new belief. Project yourself five years into the future and imagine how much joy, fulfillment, and satisfaction the new belief allowed you to experience in each of the areas of your life you listed. Now project ten years and twenty years.

7

ADOPTING POWERFUL BELIEFS

That last chapter was a lot of hard work!

I don't know how much time you invested in answering those questions, but I guarantee that it will be one of the most fruitful activities you have ever done. By getting rid of limiting beliefs and replacing them with empowering ones, your outlook will definitely be changed.

We're going to close this section with a little fun. I want you to look at the people in your life whom you admire and then go find out their belief systems. Talk to them and learn what they are doing and thinking to produce the results in their lives that you would like to see in your life.

For instance, choose a couple whose marriage both you and your spouse admire. Maybe it is your pastor and his wife, or someone you work with, or a relative, or even your own parents. Invite them out to dinner and ask them if they would mind sharing some of their beliefs concerning love and relationships, marriage, and serving others. I am sure they will be thrilled to share these things with you and to encourage you in your marriage. If they truly have an incredible marriage, they will want you to have that kind of relationship as well.

They will be honored that you asked. Not only will they enjoy the free meal, but the good fellowship as well!

Make some notes from your time together and put them into your journal. Begin adopting their beliefs into your life and it will begin empowering your marriage. At the same time, begin searching for experiences in your own past that will support those ideas. This will give you some additional supporting legs to strengthen those beliefs.

Go beyond just asking the couple *what* their beliefs are and also find out *how* they formulated such beliefs. Their answers will also be additional references for you. Even though it happened to them, you have witnessed it working in their marriage. This will serve as an additional reference point (leg) for turning the idea (table top) into a solid belief that the same will happen in your marriage. So don't forget to ask them how they came to believe the way they do.

For instance, one of their core beliefs about marriage and love could be, "*If you always put the other person first, your needs will ultimately be met as well.*" Ask them how they know that to be true?

Perhaps they will say initially they didn't believe that, but the Bible tells us to serve others, so they acted on it and found it to be true. Then they will give you all these great examples that will be wonderful references to add to your tabletop.

Do that not only with marriage, but in other areas too.

Find those whom you admire in their Christian walk, or in business, or whatever area it is that you want your belief systems to be stronger so you can live your purpose better in that particular area. Perhaps someone exhibits a skill that you want to have, such as being a great public speaker or they show empathy when others are in need.

Have some fun with this, treat some folks to dinner, and build relationships that will inspire you to live with purpose.

1.   What couple will you "interview" about their marriage belief systems? When you will you approach them?

2.   What did you learn from them? What specific belief systems did they have that you will adopt?

3.   Who else will you interview and learn powerful beliefs from? What area of your life will be enhanced by adopting this

person's belief system? Once you meet with them, write down their beliefs here.

VALUES

8

YOUR HIGHEST VALUES

In this chapter, you will begin to evaluate what is most important to you. You will start by making a list of the things you value most in your life, in order of their priority. I've given you room for ten items, but if you have more or less, that is just fine. This is your life! List as many or as few as you want.

After you have a master list of your highest values, we will test their priority to determine which ones truly are most important to you. You might get some surprises as we go through this process. We often throw out a list of priorities, but once they are put to the test and we are forced to prioritize, we discover the true desires of our heart.

When you make the first list, do not spend too much time thinking about it, just start listing the things that come to mind. We will get more specific in ranking them in Step Two.

For now, simply start with a list of the things you consider most important in your life.

STEP A: Make your list in the left hand column.

My Values	My Values Prioritized
1.	1.
2.	2.
3.	3.
4.	4.
5.	5.
6.	6.
7.	7.
8.	8.
9.	9.
10.	10.

STEP B: You are now going to test the order of importance you assigned to each item on your list.

1.   If you had to give up just one item from your list, which one would you remove? Cross that item off the list on the left and place it in the lowest open slot on the right. If you had ten items, then the first one you cross off on the left will become #10 on the right, regardless of what number it was on the left. (Note: You might be surprised to find that when you are faced with deleting something, that you are more willing to remove an item you listed as number four or five than something you had listed as

number ten.)

2.   Repeat the process until every item on the left has been moved to the list on the right.

Congratulations! You now know which of your highest values is *most* important to you.

If you want to probe a little deeper, write each value on a separate piece of paper. Beginning with the value ranked lowest on your list, crumble each paper one at a time and throw it away or shred it. If you are unwilling to throw them away in the order of your priority list on the right, you may, need to reorder them again.

When you are faced with the last two pieces of paper representing your two highest values, and you have to choose one to shred, you will know for sure what is most important to you.

Not easy, is it?

Now that you have your reordered list, it's time to take it one step forward and find out if the desired values on your Master List are actually being reflected in the way you live your life.

What are you spending the most time doing? What are you spending the most time thinking about? Where do you invest most of your energy, money, and focus? Are your actions helping you to achieve your desired values or are they leading you in the opposite direction?

You have one life to live, where are you investing

that life?

In this step you are going to rank your values according to what you are actually spending most of your time doing. These are your Actual Values and may not line up with your Desired Values. They are not based on what you *wish* was receiving most of your attention, but what your life actually reflects.

You are going to find conflict here. The first time I did this, I was shocked. I value God most and my family second, but what I found was that although those were the areas I *desired* to invest my life, most of my time and energy was actually going into my career. I did not value my career as much as I valued those other things. So, I had to work on changing where I was spending my focus, time, and energy.

You are probably going to go through the same kind of conflict. It may be a little painful at first, but keep going. Getting your two lists to match appropriately is part of learning to live and fulfill your purpose.

Take some time and create another list of your values on the next page, but reorder the list according to the activities that are currently receiving most of your time, energy, money, and focus. In the next chapter you will compare these two lists and work on activities that help you to cause your Actual Values to be more like your Desired Values.

My Actual Values *(As reflected by your actions)*

1.

2.

3.

4.

5.

6.

7.

8.

9.

10.

9

STRENGTHENING YOUR VALUES

How did you do comparing your desired values with your actual values? If you are like most normal human beings, you realized that your greatest desires are not the things you are actually spending most of your life doing. In fact, you may have even had to add some new items to your actual values list that are not even on your list of desired values at all. These things are occupying a lot of your time, energy, and focus, even though they are not reflective of your highest priorities.

Would you like to make some changes to your actual values so they mirror your desired values?

Perhaps *family* is very high on your desired values, but once you measured your time, energy, money, and focus, you realized that family was ranking sixth or seventh, instead of first or second. Or, perhaps you desired *relaxing entertainment* to be ninth or tenth, but when you measured your time, energy, money, and focus, you found that it was actually coming in around third or fourth—ahead of some of your higher values.

In order to motivate yourself to spend less time

enjoying entertainment and more time on one of your higher desires, (i.e. family time, service to others, career, etc.) you must find a way to associate more pain with the value that needs to be brought down in rank and more pleasure with the one that needs to be brought up.

Too Much of a Good Thing

For me, *relaxing entertainment* was one of my problems. It ranked way too high on my Actual Values list. When I realized how much time I was actually spending watching movies or playing video games, I found that it was occupying too much of my life. I had to create pain with that activity so I could change my habits and get busy on the things that I really did value more.

First, I began by writing down all the negative things that would result if I continued spending so much time on entertainment. Here's what I wrote:

Waste of my time. Feeds my brain with useless information and trash. Causes my children to feel unimportant because I'm watching a movie instead of spending time with them. Keeps me up too late so I can't get up early for my hour of power. Keeps me from having my quiet time. It's passive rather than active. Makes me a drone. Prevents me from being successful. Makes me normal—part of the crowd. Prevents me from being physically fit. Makes me lazy. Causes discomfort and division in my household.

All these things are true. It does not mean we never watch a movie, or that all entertainment is bad. I still love watching movies with my family. It simply means that if I want to live my purpose, I must find a way to move it down on my list (unless being a movie critic is part of my purpose!).

The best way I've found to accomplish this is to ratchet up the pain associated with the activity that needs to be moved down the list. After measuring those negatives, I might decide one movie a week is not going to take away from those other things; or, I could choose to watch a movie with the whole family instead of just watching a movie by myself or with my buddies.

You should do the same in your life. Determine which actual values are ranked too high and create a realistic list of negative results from spending so much time doing that. You will move it down the list by changing the amount of time you spend on that activity.

MORE of a Great Thing

Do the exact opposite with those values that are scoring too low. List all the great benefits from investing in the desired value. For instance, when I don't have my daily time with God, it costs me. There are negative outcomes when I don't spend that quiet time with the Lord and allow Him to help me plan my day. I needed to create a list that would help me to focus on the benefits of spending more time with God each day. Here's the list I created:

I have peace of mind. I draw closer to God. I gain more knowledge about the Bible. His laws are embedded on my heart and mind. I am able to draw from the wisdom of His Word in making my decisions. I'm guarded from temptation. I'm filled with His Spirit. I'm prepared for Battle. I'm more focused. I'm in tune with my purpose and mission. I'm confident in my leadership abilities for my family. I'm effective in any task taken on today. I no longer feel overwhelmed. I no longer feel lazy. I'm disciplined. I'm consistent. I'm at the top of my game. I'm among the elite. I'm knowledgeable about world events. I'm knowledgeable about history. I'm gaining perspective and input from a variety of sources. I'm a prolific reader. I'm continuing to learn. I'm a master of my emotions. I'm a great communicator. I'm earning my families respect. I'm setting an example. I'm filling the gaps in my learning that in the past caused insecurities. I'm preparing myself for leadership at a higher level.

When I pile up the benefits of having a consistent, daily time with God—my hour of power as I call it—it inspires me to be more diligent in that area. Later, when I evaluate my Actual Values against my Desired Values my hour of power is moving up on the Actual Values list, and the relaxing entertainment is moving down. This change comes about because of how I stacked up the negatives and positives in my mind.

You can do the same. Finish this chapter by making the same kind of lists in each of those areas of your life that need to be aligned. Once you've completed that, do the balance sheet at the end of this chapter. Go through this balance sheet on each area of your life. Be honest with yourself about the areas that need improvement, as well as the areas where you are doing well. This is what Zig Ziglar called "*a check up from the neck up.*"

This will help you to determine if you are unbalanced in any area of your life. Maybe you will find that you are spending too much time on the physical and not enough on the financial. Or too much time on the spiritual. Yes, you can be too heavenly minded to be any earthly good. I don't think God intends for us to remain in our prayer closet all day, every day of the year. Yes, you should constantly be in contact with the Lord, but you also have to go and do what He has planned for you each day.

You have to do things for the Lord while you are here. Like John Hancock said:

> "*I urge you by all that is dear, by all that is honorable, by all that is sacred, not only to pray, but to act.*"

1.   Pick a value that is scoring too high on your Actual Values results and start listing every negative you can think of that will result from spending too much time, energy, money, and focus on that value.

2.   Pick a value that is scoring too low on your Actual Values results and start listing every positive benefit you can think of that will result from spending more time, energy, money, and focus on that value.

Controlling what you link pain and pleasure to will greatly affect your destiny!

FINDING BALANCE

1.   How would you describe your rules and standards for being satisfied? Answer this question for each of the major areas of your life.

2.   What has to happen for you to feel like you're doing well in the area of family?

3.   What has to happen for you to feel like you're doing well spiritually?

4.   What has to happen for you to feel like you're doing well mentally?

5.   What has to happen for you to feel like you're doing well physically?

6.   What has to happen for you to feel like you're doing well in your career?

7.   What has to happen for you to feel like you're doing well financially?

8.   What has to happen for you to feel like you're doing well in your community?

On the next page is a personal balance sheet scorecard. Give yourself a descriptive grade on each of these seven major areas of your life. Be honest. Treat it like an accounting form with debits and credits. Under each heading put the pros on the left (what you're doing well) and put the cons on the right (what needs improvement). Change the subcategories to whatever is important to you.

PERSONAL BALANCE SHEET

SPIRITUAL
PRAYER LIFE   BIBLE STUDY

TITHES/OFFERINGS   WITNESS

FAMILY
SPOUSE   KIDS

PARENTS/GRAND   OTHER

MENTAL
READING   MEMORY

NEW SKILLS   OTHER?

PHYSICAL
WEIGHT   ENERGY

NUTRITION   HEALTH/VIBRANCY

FINANCIAL

DEBT   SAVINGS

PHILANTHROPY   SECURITY

CAREER

MAJOR MILESTONES   TEAM BUILDING

CO-WORKERS   OTHER?

COMMUNITY

FRIENDS   NEIGHBORS

SERVICE TO OTHERS   OTHER?

Use this scorecard to guide you as you improve in the areas where you feel work is needed.

PASSION

10

DISCOVERING YOUR PASSION

This is my favorite part of this whole process. Discovering your passion—the thing you love to do—and finding a way to be able to do it for a living. Actually moving your career into an area that you are passionate about is an exciting transformation!

A recent article in Forbes Magazine said only 19% of people are satisfied with their jobs. This was a survey conducted in the United States and Canada. Do you realize that means that less than one out of five people are satisfied with their jobs? Another 16% answered that question by saying, "somewhat satisfied." Two-thirds were not happy at their work. In fact, between 28-56% of a larger survey conducted worldwide said that people wanted to leave their jobs.

In this book's Introduction, I mentioned Henry David Thoreau's quote, "*most men lead lives of quiet desperation.*" What a tragedy that most people are stuck in a job they hate, in a career for which they have no passion, and from which they receive no joy.

I can't imagine living an entire life that way.

My father always said, *"Life is too short to waste it doing anything other than that for which God created you to do."* A line from the movie *Braveheart* also speaks to this, *"every man dies, not every man really lives."*

In our *One Life to Give* DVD, we asked a similar question, *"For what would you give your one life?"* Your answer to that question reveals your passion and your purpose. We're looking for the things that really give you joy and pleasure.

I love this quote from Olympian Eric Lydell, (he is the runner whose life was documented in the movie *Chariots of Fire*) he said, *"I believe God made me for a purpose and when I run I feel His pleasure."*

Can you imagine feeling God's pleasure as you live your life each day? Have you found anything in your life that has caused you to have that same sense of deep fulfillment? Can you say, as Eric Lydell did, that you believe God made you for this purpose and when you are fulfilling it, you *"feel His pleasure?"*

You were created to do something for God. You may not know what it is yet. That is why you are going through this process. There is something within you that is drawn to a particular purpose. That purpose is out there right now and it needs your heart and your passion. Your heart will identify with that cause and you will burn with passion to accomplish it, once you are connected to it.

John Wesley said, *"If you catch on fire with enthusiasm, people will come from miles around to watch you burn."* His purpose caused him to travel by horseback, preaching two or three times a day, over 40,000 sermons in his lifetime. Finding his passion and fulfilling his purpose led to The Great Awakening that happened during his lifetime. Without John Wesley and George Whitfield, there may have never been a great awakening and very likely would have been no American Revolution.

Do you want to have that same passion? Do you want to be so on fire with enthusiasm that people come from miles around to watch you burn? Not so you can be famous, but so you can live with purpose and have a positive impact on the people around you.

As you answer the questions over the next few pages of this chapter, you may find your answers have nothing to do with your current job. Your inspiration may be totally unrelated to what you are doing right now. It might not be the things others have convinced you to do. It may not even be the things *you* thought you should do.

I was trained to be a lawyer. I thought that was what I wanted to do. I thought that my passion was the law. I went to law school, started practicing law, and was about as uninspired as I could possibly be. I was simply not driven to do the daily part of practicing law. I did not enjoy it even the slightest bit.

There are droves of people out there doing the exact

same thing. Whether an attorney, CPA, business executive, whatever career they are in, it just is not their passion.

Others are passionate to practice law, or lead a business, or even crunch numbers. I cannot relate to it, but some people do, and it is great when they do.

That's what makes it so amazing to live in a nation where we are free to choose our career. We are free to find the area that we can be passionate about and serve others in that place. We bless other people with our product or service when we are passionate about what we are doing. That is why the free market works so well.

In this chapter, you will begin to look for your passion. You may already know what it is, but the process you are about to go through is going to help you zero in on that passion and truly get in touch with what it is.

You may already be doing the very thing about which you are most passionate. Perhaps you've been doing it for so long that you have lost some of your fire. As you go through this process, it will help you to once again identify with, and get excited about, what you are doing.

1.   **Think of a specific time when you felt truly inspired and take yourself back to that moment. Describe exactly what it was that made it so inspiring—get it all down on paper.**

a. What were you seeing?

b. What were you hearing?

c. What were you feeling?

d. What were you thinking?

e. What were you doing?

2. How was this moment related to the passion and purpose of your life?

Now, list four more times in your life when you felt truly inspired and answer the same questions above, for each of those times.

11

UNINSPIRING MOMENTS

Really? A chapter about how to be *UN*inspired?

Well, just as you want to move towards those areas about which you are passionate, it is a good idea to steer away from those areas that rob you of your passion.

From the last chapter, you now have a list of five times in your life when you felt truly inspired. For each of those specific moments in time, you have identified what was happening at the time. You will expand on this process a little later.

The next exercise is one that will not be quite as much fun, but it is just as important.

In this chapter we are going to think about times when you felt the most un-inspired. It happens to everyone. I mentioned in the previous chapter how I began my career practicing law and I did not enjoy it. I was not inspired by it. Having to research some obscure area of the law was no fun for me. All I wanted to do was argue my point in front of a courtroom, or teach it to someone else, but having to dig in and do the research myself was totally uninspiring.

Another time I felt very uninspired was certain moments when I was serving as a state representative.

There were times as a legislator that I was truly inspired—I loved discussing new ideas and filing a bill on some new issue. I loved to debate on the house floor. I loved taking on the opposition. All those things inspired me greatly when I was doing them.

But there were other times when I had to sit and listen to some issue that just simply was not interesting to me at all. It was not an area for which I had passion, like an obscure parks land regulation or something along those lines.

Try sitting through nine hours of committee hearings on some subject you care nothing about—that's uninspiring! It was one of those things that caused me to really think about whether or not I wanted to continue to serve in that capacity.

In the legislature, you have to deal with thousands of issues, not just the one or two about which you are passionate. So I had to decide whether it was serving in the legislature that was my passion, or if it was the particular issues that excited me.

For me, having a voice on the issues I am most passionate about outweighed all the rest. I have been able to channel that passion much more effectively as an author, speaker, & radio host, than I ever could have as a legislator.

Think about some of the things in your life that

have been uninspiring so that you can find ways to avoid having to spend time in that particular area, if at all possible. Or you can find ways to identify with why that area is necessary, even though it might be uninspiring. Sometimes, uninspiring actions are necessary in order to get to the actions that *are* inspiring.

Just as we did with the moments of inspiration in your life, I want you to think about moments when you were most *un*inspired.

One rule before you begin: you are not allowed to use an example such as sitting in a drivers-education course all day. Most of us would feel the same way in that circumstance. I want you to think of your life and recall a time when you were the most uninspired, and just as we did in the last chapter, I want you to put yourself back into that moment and write it all down. Repeat the process two more times. It is important to know which things really tap into your passion and which ones do no.

1.   Think of a specific time when you felt totally *un*inspired and take yourself back to that moment. Describe exactly what it was that made it so uninspiring—get it all down on paper.

a.   What were you seeing?

b.   What were you hearing?

c.   What were you feeling?

d.   What were you thinking?

e.   What were you doing?

2.   How is this moment related to the passion and purpose of your life? (Note: It might not have been related at all, which means you want to begin to direct your life plan in another direction. Or, though uninspiring, this may have been a necessary part of your being able to realize your passion and purpose. Later we will take a look at what we need to do to become inspired for those uninspiring but necessary times.)

Now, go back and list two more times in your life when you felt truly *un*inspired and answer the above questions for each of those times.

12

THE SWEET SPOT

You now have on paper some of the most inspiring and uninspiring moments of your life. These lists will help you to live a life of passion and purpose.

Notice that you have not yet been asked anything about making the most money. We will get to the financial side of things a little later.

One certain way of living an *un*inspired, *dis*passionate life is to set your goals simply on making money. Too many people miss their passion because they do not think they can make a living pursuing that passion.

I love talking. My wife might say I talk too much, but I love to talk. I especially love talking about cultural issues and how to be successful at impacting the world around us.

I still have to pinch myself when I consider the amazing fact that I now get paid to do that every day of my life. I get to speak and talk about what I love. I get to have great conversations with David Barton on the radio almost every day. I get to speak in front of crowds of people in arenas that are hungry for knowledge about the constitution or other topics that I cover.

The point is, I get to do what I love, what inspires me most, *and* I get paid for it!

Now you might say, I like to talk too but nobody's going to pay to listen to me. I would say to that, *"How do you know?"* How do you know that there is not a topic about which you could become an expert and then people interested in that topic would pay you to speak about it?

Josh Hamilton loves playing baseball and he gets paid quit handsomely to hit those homeruns. My pastor loves teaching about the Bible and applying it to our lives. Our church takes good financial care of him as he serves our congregation.

There are even people who get paid to shop! Yes, to go shopping! Others get paid to shoot guns all day long. The list goes on and on.

Now you may think, *"I can't blast homeruns like Josh Hamilton, or teach from the Bible,"* but there *is* some activity that you love doing and that you could make a living doing.

It may not turn out to be your first choice. If your passion is basketball and you are height-challenged (i.e., short!) like me, and you could not reach the rim of a basketball net even with help, then it is probably not likely that you will be able to make a living *playing* basketball.

However, there are hundreds of other ways to be around basketball and be part of that world. You might be gifted as a coach, sportscaster, sport's agent, security guard, arena architect, or even potentially a team owner.

The other night I was watching Tony Robbins interview Mark Cuban on a cable channel talk show and I found it interesting to hear how the billionaire wonder boy who made a ton of money selling broadcast.com for over $5 billion in his twenty's, ended up buying the Dallas Mavericks. For the last ten years, the team has been his main focus, although he's involved in a lot of other businesses too. He took the Maverick's from being a losing team to national champions. Although Cuban and I don't agree on a lot of things, he said something interesting in that interview. He said he loved sports and wanted to play sports but he was not a good enough athlete to be able to do it for a living, but he discovered that he was really good at business. So he was able to merge what he loved with what he could do well.

That makes a lot of sense. That is what I call the "sweet spot." It's that perfect place on the baseball bat. When it makes contact with the ball just right, there is magic!

You may find that within your area of passion (i.e., sports, music, faith, etc.), there could be a way for you to use some of the skills that you have to also have a career in the field you love.

In this chapter, you are going to take time to pursue this idea by making a list of some of the things that you love doing, and then following that with another list comprised of some ways you might be able to earn a living doing what you love.

Of course, some of these ideas may turn out not to be practical or possible in terms of being paid to do them, but do not give up! As you keep going through the list you will find that some concepts are going to turn out to be possible, and one of them is going to become an "ah-ha" moment where you suddenly realize that this thing you love to do does, in fact, have the potential of a career.

Now, it may mean making less money than what you are currently doing. Or it may mean making less money than what you might have the potential of making at some other job.

Would you rather have more money and be like the two-thirds of the public who want out of their jobs?

Or, would you rather make a little less money while enjoying what you do every day? When you find the sweet spot, you want to go to bed late and get up early so you can give it more and more. There is absolutely nothing wrong with making less money if you are doing what you are passionate about.

NOTE: I am *not* suggested that you foolishly pursue some "dream" and not provide for your family. Your first responsibility is to provide for your family and take care of your commitments, whether you enjoy the job necessary to do those things or not.

When I started speaking I made far less than I did as a lawyer. In fact, I spoke for free for years. I made the choice that I would rather do what I love and make less money, than to do something that I had no passion for but made more money. Today, I make more money speaking than I could make practicing law, but it's because I went after what I loved and you can do the same. Don't be afraid to dream about what it could possibly be.

NOTE AGAIN: I still had to practice law to pay the bills while I was speaking for free. So again, do NOT put your family on welfare to pursue your passion!

Remember, you are not going to have a perfect mission statement the first time you go through these exercises. You need to think of this as research. You are drawing these things out of yourself like pieces of a puzzle that will begin to fit together, over time.

The next exercise is to think about a few things you do extremely well. Think about two or three activities that you are very good at doing. I don't mean that you are just average. I'm talking about real talent. People tell you that it is an area in which you are outstanding or extraordinary.

The word extraordinary means EXTRA ordinary, beyond ordinary, or not normal. So whatever this particular activity or skill is, whether athletic, musical, communication, management, creativity, etc., it has to be something where you stand out.

Make a list of at least two or three things at which

you perform very well, and that people admire and comment on when you engage in the activity. Zig Ziglar said, *"You are the only person on earth who can use your ability."*

God has given you that gift and talent. Someone else may be able to do something similar to what you can do, but you are the only one who can use the talent that God gave to you. This is the time to think soberly about what your abilities are. Romans 12:3 says,

> *For I say, through the grace given to me, to everyone who is among you, not to think of himself more highly than he ought to think, but to think soberly, as God has dealt to each one a measure of faith.*

Most people read this Scripture and believe it means that you are not supposed to think highly of yourself, or even to think of yourself at all! Even if you are great at something, you are not supposed to think of yourself as being that good.

I do not believe that is what Paul meant at all. What he says is that you should not think more highly than you ought. Do not give yourself more credit than you deserve, or think that you are talented in an area that you just simply aren't.

You are to think soberly and reasonably about what you truly are gifted to do, according to the measure of faith that God has dealt to every man.

God has given you certain talent and He's given you the ability to recognize that talent. So that is what we are doing with this exercise. Think of those things at which you are extremely good, that you show promise in doing, and that most people recognize as exceptional when you do it.

1. Make a list of ten to twenty things that you love doing. Then list ways you could possibly earn income by participating in that activity.

1.	11.
2.	12.
3.	13.
4.	14.
5.	15.
6.	16.
7.	17.
8.	18.
9.	19.
10.	20.

2. List at least three things you are very good at doing. These are things that you do so well, people comment on it whenever you do it.

3. Is there any crossover between your lists in #1 and #2?

PURPOSE

13

LIFE MISSION STATEMENT

You have made a lot of progress already. You've discovered your identity, looked at your core belief systems, started getting rid of limiting beliefs and strengthening empowering beliefs, analyzed your values, began working on aligning your desired values with your actual values, discovered your passion and what truly inspires you, and now we are going to take all of that information and put it together into your life mission.

God has given you a purpose; perhaps He has given you several choices. He has put you here to live more abundantly, not just to exist. He wants you to be the difference maker in somebody's life, maybe even thousands or millions of lives. However, if you ignore your passion and purpose, and you just float through life, He'll use somebody else to get the job done.

You must have a clear vision and strategy for how you are going to live your purpose. That's where your mission statement comes in. It will help to keep you on track. You don't have to get depressed if you don't have one already. It takes time to develop this plan, and it is a work in progress.

The activity you are going to do in this chapter is to write your life mission statement. Your mission statement is going to change and evolve over time. You'll begin to perfect it as you get better at identifying your belief systems, identity, passions, and purpose. This is not something that happens overnight. I spent ten years getting on the right track, putting all these things in place. Hopefully, you can do it a lot faster than I did, because you can learn from some of the things that we are covering in this book.

Stay on Target

Remember at the end of the very first Star Wars movie when Luke Skywalker is making the bombing run on the Death Star? Even with all the chaos around him, that voice over the radio just kept saying *"stay on target, stay on target."*

Your mission statement is that voice for you. It is the clear direction for your life and allows you to measure everything that comes along against your mission statement. Every opportunity, every distraction; in fact, everything that is offered to you will be measured by your life mission statement.

If an activity is not going to further your mission, or if it does not serve your mission, you have to pass. That means you may need to say no to some good things in order to get to the great things that God has for you.

Worth the Effort

But your mission is not going to suddenly appear in cursive writing on the wall of your living room. It has to be developed over time through prayer and preparation. Most people tend to do the prayer part, but they ignore the preparation. That is why I wrote this book. I believe everyone has a passion deep inside; and in its purest form, that passion was placed there by God.

We already looked at the desires of our hearts and how God places those within us. Those passions will lead us to His purpose for our lives. To find your purpose and fulfill it, you have to be willing to seek and be prepared for what you will find.

As I have mentioned before, I believe God gives us a choice of whether we will fulfill our purpose or not. If you refuse or ignore your highest purpose, I think He allows other options. Like the illustration about the temperature gauge we looked at previously. If you were meant to live at 80 degrees, but you set the thermostat to 72 degrees and choose to live there instead; God will still let you serve, but you could have been living a much higher purpose.

My father describes it as the difference between God's perfect will and His *permissive* will. If you are in His perfect will, you are fulfilling your highest purpose. It's that sweet spot, almost effortless, because you enjoy being there so much. It's back to what Eric Lydell said about feeling

God's pleasure whenever he is in that purpose for which God had created him.

God's permissive will still brings Him glory, you'll still be serving Him, but it will not be in your greatest capacity. You want to live in His perfect will, and allow His perfect plan and your greatest fulfillment to unfold.

I speak from experience. I know what it is like to be in His permissive will. I spent years out of His perfect will. There have been times when I got off on a distraction that I *thought* was an opportunity, but it was not part of my life's mission or purpose. It was a good thing, yes, but it wasn't the best thing that He had for me.

If you have done the same, try doing what I did. Put it behind you. Remember, it is in the past. The past does not equal the future. From this point on, determine to do your best to seek God's perfect plan for your life.

It is much more difficult to pursue His perfect will than His permissive will. You can pretty much just let things happen and still be in His permissive will. His perfect will, however, takes cooperation and effort on your part.

Do you want to live in God's highest purpose for your life? Do you want to live an abundant, extraordinary life?

To do extraordinary things you have to be willing to spend more time, work harder, sweat more, think more, plan more, execute more, go farther than 99.9% of the people around you. You have to be willing to do what most other people are just not willing to do.

If you are only willing to do what most other people do, then you are going to live the same average life that they do. If you are willing to raise your standards and set your heights on higher ground then you will set yourself apart.

You can be extraordinary in that perfect will, living your highest purpose.

The real question is: Where do you set your standards? Are you willing to spend the time every day within your purpose? Are you willing to spend time with God in His Word and in your life plan.

Do you settle for less simply because your standards are set too low? If you set your standards at an average level, then you will live an average life. The first step in living the overcoming, conquering, extraordinary life is to set overcoming, conquering, extraordinary standards for yourself.

As you are working through this *Leader's Edge: Living Your Purpose*, I hope that you have already done the *Leader's Edge: The Power of Purposeful Communication*. If you have not, you must! It will help you to realize that the language you use not only with others, but also with yourself, will have a powerful affect on your attitude towards what you are doing.

How you phrase things will help you raise your standards. For instance, it's not what you *can* do, it's what you *will* do. Most people are complacent. They settle for less in their daily lives. When you settle for less in your daily life, you settle for less in your destiny. So if you want a fulfilled purpose, if you want to take what God has given you and live His highest purpose for your life, then every day you have to raise the standard and not settle for less that what He wants for your life. Daily you must raise your standards.

Extraordinary living means that you must do extraordinary things and take extraordinary actions, even in the little things. If you do, you will live an extraordinary life.

To set your standard, you have to develop your personal Life Mission Statement. You have to understand what your current identity is and as you are developing and empowering that identity, you will be able to modify your life mission and bring it in line with the empowered identity that you really want to have. As you take all those character traits we looked at earlier and begin embedding them into your identity, it will be easier to move your life statement into the category of His highest purpose for your life. It all works together.

That's why you have to keep coming back and working through the book. As you are constantly tweaking and improving, it is the mission statement that will keep you on track. Your life mission statement keeps you congruent with what God has for you. Your mission statement will give you a frame of reference that will link you with your identity.

Every business has a mission statement. They do this to be sure they stay on track. We need personal mission statements, as well.

A Mission Statement Example

Before you begin writing your statement, I want to share my mission statement from my life plan with you, as an example. I have a personal mission statement and a family mission statement.

PERSONAL MISSION STATEMENT

I, Rick Green, hereby declare before myself, others, and God that my primary purpose in life is to:

Fulfill God's perfect will for my life by serving others with inspiration, value, and leadership through family, speaking, writing, and public service; while receiving tremendous satisfaction, wealth, and joy.

THE GREEN FAMILY MISSION STATEMENT

With joy, the Green Family will honor and glorify God with all our hearts, minds, bodies, and souls as we strive to share the truths of Christ while influencing the course and culture of America.

We have our family statement framed and hanging in our home to help us always remember who we are and what we are doing. We took a lot of time, about a year, developing our family mission statement. We wanted it to cover every part of our lives and make sure that what we were doing in our careers, and with our family was tied together with our faith.

Our statement talks about sharing the truths of Christ while influencing the course and culture of America, but it starts with the words, *"with joy."* We did that on purpose because we found that it could be very taxing and frustrating to try to stay on mission and get the job done and lose our joy in the process. We figured that was not a good plan. We want to have joy in all we do. James says we are to *"count it all joy"* so we figured we could have joy whether times were good or bad.

You can do the same with your mission statements. Consider all the things that you want to see and accomplish as you create your life mission statement.

God has given you a meaningful purpose and you are learning to discover His perfect will for your life. Your purpose fulfills your passion and uses your unique gifts and talents. The more strategic time you spend discovering, planning, and continually refining your mission statement, the more likely you will fulfill this mission with excellence.

What is God calling you to do for Him? How will this calling affect your family, church, community, nation, and even your world? Don't try to get it perfect. Just start brainstorming. Write whatever comes into your heart and mind. Get it down in your life plan.

Remember, each of us has one life to give. For what will you give your one life? What is going to be the epicenter of your life? What is it about your life mission and your purpose that can be meaningful not only for you, but for generations to come. Begin to write your life mission today.

This will not be perfected or completed in one attempt. Simply jot down ideas and inspirations and what you already know that God has revealed to you and given you a passion to do. It will develop over time and be refined and fine-tuned for the rest of your life.

1. Each of us has one life to give. For what will you give your one life?

2. What will be the epicenter of your life?

3. What makes your purpose meaningful?

4. Every day you should remind yourself of the value of what you do.

5. As you are living this life mission and purpose, what will be some of the benefits you expect to experience?

6. As you are living this life mission and purpose, what are some of the potential downsides or negative aspects?

14

DREAMING BIG

I can still hear my mother telling me, *"You can be anything you want to be Rick, so don't dream small, make it a dream worth living."* When I was eleven years old she taught a course at my school called, *I Can*, by Zig Ziglar and Mamie McCullough. That course set me on the road that I am still traveling today. I'm grateful that from an early age I was taught that God had me here for a specific purpose, and to dream big dreams for the Lord.

What about you? Do you know your purpose? How did you do with your mission statement? Did you make a list of those things that inspire you most? Were you able to begin to put together a concept that would allow you to incorporate some of the things you are passionate about? If you are not there yet, don't worry. As you continue to work on your mission statement, the vision for your life will become clearer.

This book is called *Living Your Purpose*. You'll notice that it's not subtitled, *"…In One Day."* Living your purpose is a life-long process. It is something you will hopefully be working on for the rest of your days on earth.

If you do, you will have a powerful tool for accomplishing your purpose. Just imagine what your life plan will look like when you've been working on it every day for ten years. Imagine what it will look like in twenty years, or when you pass it on to your children or grandchildren someday. Thinking down the road like that is what helped me to dig in and do the work needed when I first got started. I wanted to be able to leave something behind for my kids and grandkids that would give them an example of how they can set their own goals in life, and live the life God has planned for them.

So, what are your goals today? Where would you like to be a year from now? How about five years from now? The older you get, the harder it may be for you to dream big and believe. Past experiences may have limited your beliefs of what God's purposes are in your life.

Perhaps you have been beaten down in the past. Or maybe you experienced some serious setbacks that are difficult to overcome. We have all been down that road at one point or another. The solution is to not allow past experiences to create limiting beliefs in the present that will affect your future.

If you are having trouble dreaming big, ask yourself why. In many cases, it may be that you are afraid to dream big because of the lingering effects of something that happened in the past. Maybe it was something you were excited about that didn't work out as planned. It did not bring the results as quickly as you hoped, and you interpreted it as a failure. The result is that now you are more cautious and tend to look for every reason why something will not work, instead of seeing the valid reasons why it will.

Too Naïve to Fail?

I remember when I started my first business. I was still in law school, but I thought I had a pretty good idea and did not want to wait to finish school before getting started. After I put my business plan together, I called my dad to tell him all about it. I was an excited twenty-year old, and my dad was (and still is) my hero. I have always valued his opinion and have the greatest respect for him. He was the best man at my wedding and is still my best friend to this day. He's been a great example and a great father.

I was excited to tell him my plan. I was sure he would be proud of me. He was a true entrepreneur and had started many companies himself. So I called him and told him my idea, but his response was not what I expected.

First, there was a long pause. Silence is not the reaction you want to be met with when you are excited. Then he asked me a simple, direct question, "*What about law school?*"

Much to my surprise, he proceeded to rattle off all the problems I could possibly face and every reason why he thought my plan would not work. My dad had been in my shoes many times. Sometimes his plans succeeded and other times they didn't. His past failures had caused him to get in the habit of always looking for the holes in a plan before jumping into a new venture.

So when I shared my idea with him, his initial response was to look for the reasons why it would not work instead of seeing the potential it had for success.

He was also trying to protect me. He did not want me to experience the pain that comes from failure. But, if you set out to look for the holes in anything, you will find them. No plan is ever perfect.

However, if you look for the potential, you will find that too. It totally depends on what you choose to focus on, and I was focused on making it work.

That conversation led to the first time in my life that my dad and I did not speak for about a month. Honestly, I was devastated. But my dream was bigger than his doubts. My naivety was exactly what was needed to make my dream a reality. My inexperience did not allow me to see the holes my father saw. So, I plunged right in. My enthusiasm was so intense I was able to overcome every obstacle that got in the way. I had maxed out every credit card I owned, used up all my law school loans, and even sold my car in a last ditch effort to launch this business.

My best friend moved in with me to help me get the business off the ground. I remember the two of us riding around Texas that hot summer in his ten-year old, beat up Nissan Sentra with no air conditioning. Not to mention the car had been wrecked by everyone in his family and every time we hit a bump, the trunk would pop open and he'd have to stop so I could jump out to close it. We were quite a sight!

Finally, on Monday October 5, 1992, (I remember it like it was yesterday) totally out of money, I sat with a bunch of friends anxiously awaiting our commercial to come on the air. We just knew the orders were going to come pouring in as soon as they saw the ad.

The orders did not exactly pour in at first. But within just a few days, things began to take off. The idea was a good one, and we ended up with half a million dollars in sales within the first six months. It was a great success for my age.

After the first hundred thousand dollars in orders, my dad had a change of heart. He realized that he had been letting his past defeats limit his vision and he turned his focus around. Within a few years he started some new companies that he would not have been willing to do without the experience that I had.

Please do not misunderstand the moral of this story. I am not at all suggesting that you ignore the advise of experienced counselors God has placed in your life. This was the only time in my life that I did not follow the advise of my father. Even to this day, his counsel heavily influences my decisions.

The Past Does Not Equal The Future

Many people allow the memory of past defeats to rule their present lives. The possible pain of failure has become greater in their minds than the potential promise of success. They move away from opportunities instead of running towards them. Even when they see that something is working for other people, they still say no. Oftentimes when this happens it is because they are judging the current situation based on past results. It is similar to the limiting beliefs that we looked at in an earlier chapter.

Experiences support ideas and cause them to become beliefs. Because something similar did not work in the past, they believe an idea will not work now.

What a shame to live your life as though the past equals the future. What would our world be like if everyone gave up after two or three, or even one hundred failed attempts?

If your child did not walk within the first ten tries, would you stop him or her from trying again? Would you put them in a chair and tell them they will never walk?

Of course not! It sounds foolish, but that is how most people approach their dreams. If it does not work out the first couple of times, they give up. They figure it just was not meant to be.

Too often, people do not get involved in a business, or become an entrepreneur, or try for a promotion at work, simply because they are trying to drive forward while

164

looking in the rear view mirror. They are judging the future entirely by the past and that does not get them far in life.

We should not spend our lives looking behind us; we must remember that the past does not equal the future.

Thomas Edison is a great example. He held 1,093 patents for things he invented, some of which completely transformed our world. Just a few of them were the phonograph, motion picture camera, and of course the electric light bulb.

When he was in school, however, his teachers told him he had "addled brains." Today, we would call it ADD or ADHD and would have put him on Ritalin. He may never have invented anything if they had that drug back in the 1860's when he was a child.

His mother refused to allow her son to be labeled. She chose to home school him instead. In the chapter on beliefs, we learned how sometimes what we believe is from what other people have told us about ourselves. Thomas Edison's mother prevented the limiting belief that he had an addled brain to become a part of his belief system.

Instead, by the time he was twelve, he had read practically every book in the library and had started his own business. By the time he was fourteen he had his own newspaper and was making money and reinvesting it into his lab in the basement of his family home.

Thomas Edison tried and failed many times, but he

never gave up. Legend has it that he tried thousands of times before he invented the light bulb. When people asked him how many times he failed, he would answer, *"I haven't failed, I have just found thousands of ways how not to invent the electric light bulb."* Today we are all benefiting from his tenacity. The past did not dictate his future. His personal willingness to charge forward and put in the time and effort necessary to complete his mission should inspire us all.

Perhaps you've heard of Colonel Sanders. He was the one who started Kentucky Fried Chicken and changed the eating habits of a nation. Today there are franchises in every city in America. Did he just get lucky? No. He failed many times. He was sixty-five when he started the business and for two years he drove around the country trying to get people to buy his recipe. He was sleeping in his car and living off of chicken, but he did not give up. Without one yes, he managed to keep trying. After 1,009 people had told him no, he finally got a yes, and the rest became history.

He did not let the past determine his future. He knew his mission. He knew his purpose and was willing to keep going.

Are you willing to do the same? Are you fulfilling your purpose?

It is important to note here that I am not suggesting you should reject all "negative" council. If everyone around you is cautioning you, and you have some uncertainty in your own heart and mind as well, you would be wise to spend some time in prayer and seeking further advice.

Don't be reckless and foolish.

On the other hand, if you have that internal assurance and you know that God has given you the ability to do something, then do not be easily discouraged. If He has given you a passion for something and an aptitude for it, then don't let the naysayers (and there will be some) get you off track.

That is why having your own mission statement is so important. It will help you stay on track when the "no's" in life try to get you off your mission. Failures will not derail you if you know your mission. Remember how Edison saw his failures as successes because he knew he was learning how *not* to do it.

No matter how many times you get knocked down, as long as you get up one more time you are still in the game. Study the lives of people in history who have kept getting back into the game. Men like Thomas Edison, Colonel Sanders, and even Abraham Lincoln, who lost elections and failed in business, but never let those things keep him down.

If fact he kept coming back and ultimately at age sixty he was elected President of the United States, and went on to end slavery in our nation and preserve our union. He fulfilled his mission because he did not give up after the defeats.

Most people accept any one defeat as a preview of their entire life. They define themselves by that defeat, and allow it to shape their identities.

If you allow that to happen, you are allowing the past to dictate the future. Don't let that happen to you! You cannot look at the past pages of your life and assume it is the definition of your future. Your future is what you make it. God has a purpose for you, and it's up to you to fulfill it.

What do you want to be? How do you want God to use you? What amount of money would you like to earn and be responsible for to God? What do you want to be able to give your family? How do you want to raise your children? Get detailed.

Over the next few chapters you are going to begin getting into the details of what you want to do and what desires you believe God has put in your heart. If you live your life knowing your purpose and planning that purpose in a detailed way and you constantly measure how you are doing, then, Lord Willing, you can achieve the desires of your heart.

In order to live your purpose, you first have to have a clearly defined mission and detailed goals that will help you make sure that everything stays congruent in your life. You must have dreams and goals that are big enough to motivate you to take the action.

If your goal is just to pay off your wife's ten-year-old car and that is the only goal you have, do you think you will be willing to get up early in the morning and go to bed late at night, and face and overcome the obstacles of success every day? Are you going to do what it takes to make that dream come true? Do you think you will be willing to do all that if your only goal is just to pay off an old car?

Not likely.

On the other hand, what if your goal is to get completely out of debt, to be able to leave your job, and never work for another man the rest of your life?

What if your goal is to be able to go wherever God leads you and not have to worry about finances? Wouldn't it be great to be able to be at every one of your kid's baseball games, or every recital? Would you like to be able to take your family around the country, or the world? Would you like to be able to contribute worthy causes and make a difference in the lives of others?

These are the kind of goals that motivate. Do you have any like this?

Imagine if you could contribute to every candidate that you thought would help to move our nation in the right direction? Or what if you had the finances to support the Alliance Defending Freedom and the Liberty Council, two great legal organizations. What would happen if you could support Patriot Academy with scholarships for students to help them learn how to fulfill their passion and purpose and make a difference in the world around them.

If your *why* is big enough, you will find the *how* to make it happen. You will figure it out. The end result has got to be bigger than the road to get there. Once you truly find motivating dreams, they will ignite a fire in you, and, as we learned from John Wesley earlier, *"If you catch on fire with enthusiasm, people will come from miles around to watch you burn."*

To catch on fire with enthusiasm, you have to have a passion and a purpose that will ignite that kind of enthusiasm within you and give you the necessary drive and ambition to keep going, no matter what obstacles you might face. You'll have the vision to see past the no's even if it is 1,009, like Colonel Sanders. You won't be afraid of failure. You'll realize that the freedom to fail is what gives you the freedom to succeed.

"Where there is no vision, the people perish" (Proverbs 29:2, KJV). If there is nothing driving you on, you are going to perish. You are going to become stagnant. It needs to be a passion that comes from deep within you, from a source that you may not even understand. It is God's way of lighting a fire in your belly. It will make you get up no matter how many times you get knocked down.

It was Vince Lombardi that originally said, *"It is not whether you get knocked down; it's whether you get back up."* Success rarely comes on the first attempt. Don't be afraid of having to get back up.

For a dream to give you that kind of fire, it has to be bigger than the bumps in the road, and it is going to take time for you to develop those kinds of dreams and set those lofty goals. That is what you are going to begin to do in the next chapter.

15

SPECIFIC GOALS

You are now going to start getting into the details by setting specific goals. I am sure you have set goals before. You probably do it every New Year's Eve, but rarely reach any of them, right?

The problem with setting goals once a year is that we don't check them until a year later. How much more likely are you to achieve your goal if you measure your progress towards reaching that goal on a monthly basis, instead of just once a year?

What if halfway through the year you were to reassess your goals and modify your actions in order to reach those goals? What if you did that once a month or once a week? What if you did that every day? Do you think you would do better and reach more of your goals that way?

This plan is designed to help you measure your goals on a daily basis. First, you will get very specific on what you really want to do. Once on paper, you can measure your progress and see if you are moving in the right direction to accomplish your goals. You will get specific about what you are looking for, and you will make sure that your current goals fit with your life purpose.

You probably already know that most people don't set goals. Only a small percentage, some studies say about 3%, actually are goal setters. Did you know that the small group of people that regularly set goals achieve more in their lives than all the others combined? Contrasting the results in the life of someone who sets goals, with someone who just floats along aimlessly, is like comparing the batting statistics of those in the Baseball Hall of Fame to the first year T-Ball team in your neighborhood. There really is no comparison!

If you do not set goals for your life and measure those goals periodically, then you are just being bounced around by whatever comes your way. You are at the mercy of circumstances, and they will control your destiny, rather than you living your purpose.

The remainder of this book is going to be about asking and answering specific questions so that you are directly setting the goals that will help you to achieve and live your purpose.

Seven Proven Steps for Achieving Goals

You can find a lot of books and programs that will help you to set and reach goals. Every bookstore is full of them. The best one I have ever used has been around for a while. Developed by Zig Ziglar, I believe it to be the best goal setting formula on the planet.

Twenty years ago, I was honored to team up with Zig in producing an audio program that outlined this program. We called it *"Seven Steps to the American Dream."* But since the cover has a picture of me with a mullet, I've worked hard to make sure all copies have been expunged from the record!

Zig's goal setting program includes a seven-step process and I encourage you to follow those seven steps for every goal you set. I've listed the seven steps below, as a quick overview, and we will get more specific later. If you have been setting goals for awhile, some of these steps may seem very basic, but all of them are important.

1. **Identify the goal.** What is it that you want?

2. **Set a deadline for achieving it.** If you don't set that deadline, you will put it off and not take the actions necessary to reach that goal.

3. **List the obstacles you have to overcome.** What are the challenges between you and achieving this goal?

4. **Identify the people and groups to work with in order to achieve the goal.**

5. **List the skills, knowledge, and things you need to learn that are required to reach the goal.**

6. **Develop your plan of action.** That is what this whole process of daily going through your life plan is all about. It's not enough to discover your goals, you've got to have a plan of action and execute the plan.

7. **List the benefits.** This will motivate you to reach that goal. This is your *why* for the goal. If you are constantly in tune with the benefits of reaching that goal then you have to identify more than just what the goal is by why you want to reach that goal. Oftentimes it is the answer to why that is the real goal.

Finding the Why for Each Goal

Everything you want goes beyond the materialistic things or the circumstances around you. What you truly want, when you really get down to it, is a feeling. There is a specific feeling that we get when we reach our goals.

For instance, people do not want money so they can have pieces of paper with dead presidents' pictures on them. It is not the physical money they want. It is what the money allows them to do. It might give the feeling of security, comfort, pride, confidence, etc. Or maybe it buys something like a house, car, or clothes that in turn gives the same kind of feeling. A dream house may give a person a sense of love or family, prestige, or maybe security.

It will be different things to different people, because we do not all have the same associations with homes or money. So you must identify the why of your certain goals.

I cannot tell you what the *why* will be for you, only you can define that. If you want real motivation, you must get past listing the *things* you would like, i.e. a car, a house, a college degree, and start digging into finding out *why* you want those things.

If you ask yourself why you want a particular goal and the answer is not a feeling, dig a little deeper. Keep asking what reaching the goal will give you until the answer is a feeling. No matter what you list as your dream or your goal, the reason you want that goal is going to boil down to a feeling, if you dig deep enough.

I used to think I wanted a convertible sports car. In my twenty's, that was one of my goals. I wanted a convertible sports car and I thought I wanted it just to have one. Then I finally got one, and I figured out that what I really wanted was to go really fast and look really cool. That was the why of my goal. That was the feeling that I wanted. I wanted to feel cool and I got that from that car. As I got older, the rattles and wind noise of a convertible became far more annoying than the "coolness" when the top was down and I have had a pickup truck ever since!

For each of your goals, find out what the *why* is for you.

For a long time I had the goal of having more than 100 students attend Patriot Academy. That is our youth leadership program where we bring students in from all over the nation, ages sixteen to twenty-five. We also train adults over twenty-five on the *Citizen Track*, but High School and College students are our main focus. The goal in my life plan for years was that I would bring 100 or more students to the Capitol with me at one time.

Now, that describes the "what" of my goal, not the "why." I really do not want to be around 100 teenagers for a week. That was never my real goal. My real goal for having 100 students at Patriot Academy was so that we could impact many lives and then impact the world through their leadership.

At Patriot Academy we empower young leaders to go out and change their world. Having 100 students attend would mean we would have a lot of excitement and potential at Patriot Academy, more energy, and more of a feeling that we are part of a movement. Not just a small group of people, but a movement. That's exactly what happened when we finally broke that mark a couple of years ago and had over 100 students. We could feel the energy and excitement. For the students, I think it felt better too because they didn't feel like they were just one of a dozen, now they were part of a huge movement.

As the founder, I felt like we were achieving our goals by reaching lots of students. That gave me a feeling of significance—of impact. I felt as though we were doing something that mattered, changing lives, and leaving a legacy.

With each goal there is a reason why those goals are significant. For me, at Patriot Academy it was the feeling of contribution and making a difference in the lives of others. It was also the feeling of significance and legacy and being part of something bigger than myself, something that would last long after I'm dead. That was the *why* for me.

What's the *why* for you? Why do you want certain things? As you go through this goal setting process, you will answer questions that will help you identify the *why*.

Joy in the Journey

Why is it that God put that goal in your heart to achieve? If you know what the *why* is, you will enjoy the process because you will have a sense of purpose behind what you are doing. In this way, you will not have to wait until you reach your goal to be happy. You can be happy in the process of getting there. By tapping into the passion, the reason why you do certain things, you will perform better. You will be more successful at everything that you do.

> *Delight thyself also in the LORD, and He shall give thee the desires of thine heart. Commit thy way unto the LORD; trust also in Him, and He shall bring it to pass.* **–Psalm 37:4-5 (21ˢᵗ Cent KJV)**

> *Open up before God, keep nothing back; he'll do whatever*

needs to be done: He'll validate your life in the clear light of day and stamp you with approval at high noon. Quiet down before God, be prayerful before him. **–Psalm 37:5-7 (The Message)**

God's Word says that He will give you the desires of your heart. He will give you that stamp of approval if you are working towards the purpose that He has placed in your heart.

Matthew Henry's commentary on this verse says something extremely important for you as you set out to attain your goals. He said:

We are here counseled to live a life of confidence and complacency in God, and that will keep us from fretting at the prosperity of evil-doers; if we do well for our own souls, we shall see little reason to envy those that do so ill for theirs. Here are three excellent precepts, which we are to be ruled by, and, to enforce them, three precious promises, which we may rely upon.

1. We must make God our hope in the way of duty and then we shall have a comfortable subsistence in this world, v. 3. (1.) It is required that we trust in the Lord and do good, that we confide in God and conform to him.

2. We must make God our heart's delight and then we shall have our heart's desire, v. 4. We must not only depend upon God, but solace ourselves in him. And even this pleasant duty of delighting in God has a promise annexed to it, which is very full and precious, enough to recompense the hardest services: He shall give thee the desires of thy heart. He has not promised to gratify all the appetites of the body and the humours of the fancy, but to grant all the desires

178

of the heart, all the cravings of the renewed sanctified soul. What is the desire of the heart of a good man? It is this, to know, and love, and live to God, to please him and to be pleased in him.

4. *We must make God our guide, and submit in everything to his guidance and disposal; and then all our affairs, even those that seem most intricate and perplexed, shall be made to issue well and to our satisfaction. The duty is very easy; and, if we do it aright, it will make us easy: Commit thy way unto the Lord; roll thy way upon the Lord (so the margin reads it), Prov. 16:3; Ps. 55:22. Cast thy burden upon the Lord, the burden of thy care, 1 Pt. 5:7. We must roll it off ourselves, so as not to afflict and perplex ourselves with thoughts about future events (Mt. 6:25), not to cumber and trouble ourselves either with the contrivance of the means or with expectation of the end, but refer it to God, leave it to him by his wise and good providence to order and dispose of all our concerns as he pleases.* <u>We must do our duty (that must be our care) and then leave the event with God.</u> *We must follow Providence, and not force it, subscribe to Infinite Wisdom and not prescribe. The promise is very sweet. In general, "He shall bring that to pass, whatever it is, which thou hast committed to him,* <u>*if not to thy contrivance, yet to thy content.*</u> *He will find means to extricate thee out of thy straits, to prevent thy fears, and bring about thy purposes, to thy satisfaction."*

I believe what Matthew Henry is saying is that if a desire of your heart is aligned with your purpose, you cannot receive great reward if you have left God out of the equation.

You must have a relationship with God if you want your purpose to be fulfilling. If you want the joy and the feelings we've talked about to become a reality in your life, you need to make sure that you are living in line with the purpose that God has for you. That is the sweet spot where you will have peace.

You will be able to do your duty, do your work, set your goals, plan your purpose, work out those plans, and ultimately do your part of God's plan. All along, you will have peace in knowing that God is sovereign. He is in charge. You don't have to sweat this stuff. Just do your part. I'm not saying you sit back and do nothing. Do your duty and let God take care of the results.

It is that way with our goals. You should not set goals and then be upset if you do not reach a particular one. You should set goals as a benchmark, and constantly measure whether it fits with your purpose or not. If we have aligned our goals with what we believe in our hearts God wants us to do, then God is going to help us get there. I believe that with all my heart. He has done it throughout my life. When I am in line with the purpose He has given me, it's almost like it comes easy. I hesitate to say that, because I always encourage people to expect hard work. You are going to have to put some elbow grease in, but that hard work is so much easier to do when it is something you love doing.

I can work eighteen hours a day when I'm doing stuff that I love. But if I have to do something that I don't love, something that is outside my purpose and not in the sweet spot of God's perfect will for me, then, even five hours is too much. I'll be worn out. The difference is that when I am in the sweet spot, it does not even seem like work.

Now I'm going to ask you to get random. I want you to start writing a list of 100 goals, as fast as you can, in the space provided on the following pages. These goals can be small or big. You can mix them up between every area of your life. I just want you to list as many as you can without considering how possible each will be to achieve.

Write down everything you've ever wanted to accomplish or do. Include everything from jumping out of a plane someday (with a parachute of course) to learning Spanish, to traveling to Europe. Write every goal you can think of, and if you have more than 100 or cannot quite come up with 100, that is okay too. Keep writing as fast as you can until you cannot think of anything else. Once you get that done, begin answering the questions that follow.

"What you get by achieving your goals is not as important as what you become by achieving your goals." **- Zig Ziglar**

"The true purpose of goals is to compel you to become the person it takes to achieve them." **- Jim Rohn**

"The highest reward for a person's toil is not what they get for it, but what they become by it." **- John Ruskin**

<u>List 100 Goals (big and small)</u>

1)	21)	41)
2)	22)	42)
3)	23)	43)
4)	24)	44)
5)	25)	45)
6)	26)	46)
7)	27)	47)
8)	28)	48)
9)	29)	49)
10)	30)	50)
11)	31)	51)
12)	32)	52)
13)	33)	53)
14)	34)	54)
15)	35)	55)
16)	36)	56)
17)	37)	57)
18)	38)	58)
19)	39)	59)
20)	40)	60)

61)	75)	89)
62)	76)	90)
63)	77)	91)
64)	78)	92)
65)	79)	93)
66)	80)	94)
67)	81)	95)
68)	82)	96)
69)	83)	97)
70)	84)	98)
71)	85)	99)
72)	86)	100)
73)	87)	
74)	88)	

1. If you knew you could not fail, what would you love to be doing in five years?

2. If you knew you could not fail, what would you love to be doing in ten years?

3. If you knew you could not fail, what would you love to be doing in twenty years?

"You were born to win, but to be a winner, you must plan to win, prepare to win, and expect to win." — **Zig Ziglar**

16

MAJOR MILESTONES

At this point, you have your 100 goals listed. Some of them are big-ticket things that you would like to accomplish in the next five, ten, or twenty years. Others are smaller goals that you may reach in days.

In this chapter, focus on the goals that you would consider the most important. These are major milestones. These are the goals that once attained, will be life changers.

These may or may not necessarily be your ultimate purpose, but each is an important piece of hitting that mark. If, for instance, you are called to become a scientist or an inventor, and you need a particular degree in order to do that, then earning that degree is going to be a major milestone. Similarly, if one of your goals is to be elected Governor of your state, then a major milestone to getting there might be to first win election to the legislature or some other more local office.

Spend time thinking through the major milestones you will need to reach along your path. These are the things that are going to make a significant difference for the big dreams you have for your life. Mapping these out beforehand will keep you from spending time working towards goals that do not make sense for you. You want to be sure your goals meet the right criteria before you spend years of your life trying to accomplish them.

You also have to be sure the goal is realistically possible. Yes, I told you to dream big. But at the same time, you need to be balanced and realistic about the goals you set. For instance, I am certain that I will never land a recording contract as a singer. No matter how much I dream about it, or how hard I work on it, it will never happen, because I can't sing to save my life.

On the other hand, my wife's family is full of gifted singers. They are incredible. When I was campaigning for office, they would put on concerts before I spoke. They were so good that I could have gotten up after them and said my "A, B, C's" and still win votes. We made a pact, I don't sing and they don't give speeches. It has worked out very well over the years!

So a realistic milestone for me would not be winning *American Idol.* I would be wasting my time, money, and energy if I thought I could work hard enough to make that remotely possible. And there is no doubt I would be one of the embarrassing segments where the judges roll their eyes and the audience laughs out loud!

I'm not saying you should shoot down your big dreams. If you can see a probable or possible path to reaching that milestone, then don't nix the idea. But if it is a fairy tale, rather than a dream, then you have to recognize that it is unwise to invest years of your life working towards something that is realistically impossible, especially when there are other milestones that are realistically possible and will give you just as much joy in the end.

So, before you map out a major milestone, answer the following to see if your goals are aligned with your purpose.

1. **Does this fit into your life mission? Does it enhance your purpose, equip you better for that purpose, or otherwise allow you to fulfill your greatest goals in life?**

2. **Is it realistically possible?**

3. **How will you know when you achieve it? What is the definition of success for this milestone?**

4. **Does it violate any of your values? Does it go against what you believe? If it does, don't do it! If it's unethical or prevents you from living up to those highest desired values that you worked on earlier in the book—don't do it!**

These are the four tests for each milestone. Take the time to list some of the major milestones you need to reach.

Start by listing three or four milestones. Then pick one of those that you want to begin working through.

I'm going to use one of my milestones as an example. *Hosting Patriot Academy with 150 House members, 31 Senators, and a Supreme Court.* This was my original dream vision of Patriot Academy. We're not quite there yet. We are close with about 125 students a year coming right now. But I would like to get to this point. So this is one of my major milestones that would be a great achievement for us, and something that would reinforce that I am on the right path for what I believe is my purpose.

Here are the steps that we are going to go through for this part of the process. The first question you have to ask is:

1. **Why do you want to reach this milestone? This is the identifying of the goal, the why behind the what. So jot down some notes about why you want to achieve the milestone. This is actually a combination of steps 1 and 7 from Zig's seven steps in the previous chapter.**

2. **What is your deadline for achieving this milestone?**

3. What obstacles must you overcome to achieve this major milestone?

4. Who are the people and groups that you need to work with to achieve this milestone?

5. What skills/knowledge do you need to acquire in order to achieve this?

6. What is your plan of action for achieving this goal? This will be detailed below in the "mind mapping" portion of this process.

Go through each of the above questions for each of your milestones. Answer each question. One of the things that used to help me think about how to achieve these things and answer the questions was to think about one of my mentors or heroes and how they would set out to reach this milestone. Then I would try to model what I thought they would do.

Next, let's do the mind mapping part of reaching your milestone.

MIND MAPPING A MAJOR MILESTONE

I always start with the last step—the realization of the milestone—and then I work backwards until I get all the way to where I am today and the things I need to do now to reach the final outcome. Using the example that I have given you for Patriot Academy, this is how some of my mind mapping exercise looks:

How will I know that I have achieved this milestone? Working backwards here's what my answer is:

• I will be driving away from the Capitol at the end of Patriot Academy knowing that the 180 plus students had an incredible experience, learned powerful skills, met amazing people, and are ready to lead the change.

• For the above to happen, I will have had to conduct PA with a smooth schedule and operations, great speakers and workshops, concluding with a powerful closing ceremony.

• For the above to happen, at the beginning of the week I would have had to welcome PA students at orientation.

• For the above to happen, I would have had to meet and pray with all the volunteers beforehand, as the team is briefed prior to orientation.

• Before that I will have had to confirm all the speakers, events, locations, and activities for the week of PA15

So, you get the idea. I am just backing up in the process. These are the things that will have to happen to reach that ultimate goal.

• I will contact and schedule all speakers.
• I will plan the entire schedule for PA.
• Students are sent pre-packets.
• Students send in their tuition and applications.
• I recruit interested students.
• I prepare rough schedule for PA.
• I raise the necessary funds to conduct a successful PA.

The first action steps would be raising the money for Patriot Academy and preparing the schedule. So, what is the first and highest priority step I will need to take to achieve it? When will I do it? Etc.

Go through these questions for yourself. Once you have worked backwards, what is the first and highest priority step you need to achieve? Then identify the next few priority steps that you will need to take to achieve this major milestone. What are your measurements along the way?

Walk through all of the questions. A lot of the questions will get you thinking about and doing things you may not have done before when setting out to reach a particular goal. Logging your activity and measurements along the way to achieving this milestone, or thinking about how you will know you are on track, are essential elements to increasing your likelihood of success.

Another great question that you are going to be asked as you walk through this process is, *"Who will hold you accountable for achieving your goal?"*

And another one is, *"What are the pleasures you'll experience?"* This will bring you back to piling up the pleasures that result from taking the positive actions in reaching the goal. Then pile up the pains that inaction would cause. What pains will you experience by not achieving it? You might also have to sacrifice in some other areas to achieve this major outcome. What reward will you give yourself for achieving it? You've got to be sure that you are rewarding results, not just activity.

This is going to take time, but go through this mind-mapping process for at least one major milestone in your life before moving on to the next chapter. Over time, come back and do that for each of the major milestones that you have planned out for your life.

A lot of people say they are planning their future, but all they are doing is setting down a couple of goals and saying, "I hope I achieve that by the end of my life." The difference with our process will be seen in the results you get by actually planning. The detailed planning and taking the time to sit down and step by step write out what you will do, will make all the difference in the world. You will have so much more success in achieving your goals.

So, let's get it done. Let's do it in excellence. Do it with excitement, joy, and passion, and recognize that this is your chance to live your purpose. You are going to live your purpose because you are finally going to have it planned out and you are going to be able to accomplish these major milestones and goals in your life so that you can have a greater impact on the world around you.

1. What is the first and highest priority step you will take to achieve your major milestone? When will you do it?

Example: *To plan the week with rough schedule*

2. What are the next three priority steps you will take to achieve your goal?

3. What are the next three priority steps you will take to achieve your goal?

4. What are the measurements along the way?

5. How will you log your activity progress? (Be sure to focus on results not just activities.)

6. How will you know you are on track with achieving it?

7. Who will hold you accountable for achieving it?

8. How will achieving your major outcome help you fulfill your life purpose?

9. What pleasures will you experience achieving it?

10. What pains will you experience achieving it?

11. What reward will you give yourself for achieving it? (Be sure to reward results not just activities.)

17

SPIRITUAL

In the following chapters you are going to be looking at seven areas of your life in extreme detail: Spiritual, Family, Mental, Physical, Financial, Career, and Community.

Of the seven, I always list spiritual first because I think it is the most important. Without that part of your life being in order, everything else has no joy or meaning. If you do not think your spiritual life is as important as your financial well being, let me ask you one simple question. How much money did Sam Walton leave behind when he died? The answer is, all of it. That ought to give you a clue as to what is most important.

The spiritual aspect of your life is extremely important. The questions in this chapter are designed to help you analyze how you are doing spiritually. They are a combination of great questions that I have absorbed from a lot of folks over the years, some of whom I mentioned in the introduction.

Think through your answers. Be honest in describing your current spiritual life. Some of these questions may initially offend you and make you feel as though your faith is being challenged. I want you to challenge your faith so you will become stronger in it.

A lot of people think that because Thomas Jefferson told his nephew in a letter that he should, *"Question with boldness even the existence of God"* that Jefferson did not believe in the existence of God. That is not what Jefferson meant. If you read the letter in its entirety, you will see that what he was challenging his nephew to do was to get educated about his faith. He wanted him to study and be able to reason from the pages of Scriptures, so that he could defend his faith. This is quite clear when you read the full letter instead of taking things out of context like most anti-Christian historians do these days.

If you *do* question with boldness the existence of God, you will come to the ultimate conclusion that there is indeed a God. You do not want to just *assume* God exists because your parents believe in Him or because you were raised in the church. You want to be able to prove to others that what you know about God is true.

The following questions are challenging. The goal is to equip you to be better able to defend your faith.

Another important part of this process is for you to find a spiritual mentor. This should be someone you look up to and to whom you can go to for spiritual guidance. For me, I have both my pastor and my father. There are also a couple of other people in my life who I occasionally go to with questions. I also have an accountability partner.

Hour of Power

Another thing I really want to stress is the importance of having a quiet time—an hour of power. Some people like to have that time alone with the Lord in the morning; others prefer to spend that time with Him in the evening. I've found that it works best for me in the morning because it sets everything on the right course for the day.

When I do not have my time in the morning with God, I can tell the difference for the rest of the day. I am not nearly as effective. I do not get as much done.

That hour that you spend with the Lord each day will multiple the other hours in the day. Don't fall into the trap that sometimes I allow myself to fall into. I've even done it this week as I was meeting the deadline for finishing this book. I skipped my hour of power because I thought I did not have time. But I have no doubt much more would have been accomplished in a shorter period of time if I had stuck with my hour of power.

I have found that the more consistent I am with my hour of power, the more effective I am and the more likely I am to stay on track in every area of my life.

Your time can be whatever you want it to be. You can read first and then pray, or visa versa. You can also use fifteen minutes of that time with the Lord to work through sections of your life plan.

This has been a habit of mine since I was young, though not anywhere near as consistent as I wish it were. I remember when I was growing up we used to go to a church in Dallas, called Church on the Rock. Our pastor took us through a study in the Lord's Prayer, titled *"Could You Not Tarry One Hour?"* The lessons on prayer that I learned during that study impacted my prayer life so much that they are still part of my daily prayer time to this day. An outline of that prayer process is included at the end of this chapter.

The goal of this time is to dig deep and spend time praising God every morning and thanking Him. You might know that old song verse, *"count your blessings, name them one by one; count your blessings, see what God has done."* This is a great opportunity to thank God for each of those different areas where He is blessing you.

When you pray, *"Thy kingdom come, thy will be done ,on earth as it is in Heaven,"* set forth His kingdom in every area of your life. In your personal life, your family life, your career. In all seven areas we will be working on later, pray for His kingdom to come, His will to be done. Begin thanking God for bringing those areas in line with His purpose for your life.

As we talked about earlier, you want God's perfect will, not just His permissive will. So when you pray, *"thy Kingdom come, they will be done on earth as it is in Heaven"* you're asking God to let His will be done, not yours and to help you bring your desires in line with His will.

"Give us this day our daily bread" is when you pray for blessings for yourself, family, church, company, all of these areas. Get specific. If you have financial needs, this is the time to ask for those very specific needs.

"Forgive us our trespasses as we forgive those who trespass against us." This is a great time to ask God to give you a heart of forgiveness towards those who have wronged you in the past and those who may wrong you today.

"Lead us not into temptation, but deliver us from evil." Put on the whole armor of God, the Helmet of salvation, the Breastplate of Righteousness, Loins gird about with the belt of truth, Feet shod with the preparation of the gospel of peace, the shield of faith, and the sword of the spirit. Think about what all of those mean to you in your spiritual life.

Close by praising God. *"For thine is the Kingdom, the Power, and the glory, forever, amen."*

I encourage you liven up your prayer life with an hour of power.

Here Lies…

The last thing you will do in the questions at the end of this chapter is to write your own epitaph. I know that sounds morbid, but you are going to actually write what you would want people to say about you 100 years after your death.

If you believe setting goals while you are alive is powerful, how about setting goals for what will happen when you are gone? Many great people, world changers, fulfilled their most powerful goals after their death because of the things that they set in motion while they were alive.

John Quincy Adams is a perfect example. He worked hard, and spent seventeen years in Congress fighting to end slavery. He did not get to see it happen, but because of his work and his mentoring of Abraham Lincoln, who served one term with him, his dream was ultimately fulfilled.

How would you like to be remembered? This is your chance to write your own legacy so that you can see whether or not your purpose is aligning with all the things you are doing on a daily basis.

1. Describe the spiritual life you would love to have.

2. Who, whether living or dead, best exhibits the kind of spiritual life you would like to live?

3. What books, courses, classes, etc. do you plan to study? Make a list of each and set a goal for completing that study.

4. How would you describe your faith?

5. How did you come to join this particular faith and why did you choose it over others?

6. Who is your spiritual mentor? If none, whom could you seek out to build such a relationship?

7. For whom could you serve as a spiritual mentor and what will you teach them?

8. At what moment in life have you felt the closest to God?

9. Where and at what time do you plan to spend time alone with God each day?

10. How or what would you love a writer to write about you 100 years after your death? Imagine what this would be and then concisely write down your own *Legacy*.

DAILY HOUR OF POWER

"OUR FATHER WHICH ART IN HEAVEN. HALLOWED BE THY NAME." (Praise him for His Blessings in every area)

<u>Name</u>	<u>Translation</u>
Jehovah-tsidkenu	*"Jehovah our righteousness"*
Jehovah-m'kaddesh	*"Jehovah who sanctifies"*
Jehovah-shalom	*"Jehovah is peace"*
Jehovah-shammah	*"Jehovah is there"*
Jehovah-nissi	*"Jehovah my banner"*
Jehovah-rohi	*"Jehovah my shepherd"*
Jehovah-rophe	*"Jehovah heals"*
Jehovah-jireh	*"Jehovah's provision shall be seen"*

"THY KINGDOM COME, THY WILL BE DONE, ON EARTH AS IT IS IN HEAVEN." (This is your chance to work on aligning your desires with God's Perfect Will in each and every area of your life: Personal: *Attitude*, mind set, desires, thoughts, skills, traits, health, Family: *Immediate* and extended; *career, friends, coworkers; leaders:* community, state, local, and national)

"GIVE US THS DAY OUR DAILY BREAD." (Pray specifically for yourself, your family, your church, your company, your state, your nation, etc.)

"FORGIVE US OUR TRESPASSES AS WE FORGIVE THOSE WHO TRESPASS AGAINST US." (Forgive any who have "done you wrong" and set your heart to forgive any who "do you wrong" today. Ask forgiveness for your own "wrong doings" and know that it is forgotten as far as the east is to the west.)

"LEAD US NOT INTO TEMPTATION, BUT DELIVER US FROM EVIL." (Put on the armor of God in preparing for the day)

HELMET OF SALVATION (Take on the mind of Christ -- His thoughts, His creativity, His characteristic, His wisdom)

BREASTPLATE OF RIGHTEOUSNESS. (You have been made pure through Him)

LIONS GIRD ABOUT WITH TRUTH. (The truth shall set you free)

FEET SHOD WITH THE PREPARATION OF THE GOSPEL OF PEACE. (Be at peace knowing you are well grounded, your feet and path are sure)

SHEILD OF FAITH. (Your faith shall be your protection)

SWORD OF THE SPIRIT. (Know His Word, have it in your heart and songs of praise on your tongue)

"FOR THINE IS THE KINGDOM, THE POWER, AND THE GLORY FOREVER, AMEM." (Give Him the glory in ALL things. Know His Kingdom, His Power, and His Glory will be evident in your life.)

18

FAMILY

Have you ever wondered why American families are falling apart? You could point to a lot of different reasons, but I'm going to suggest that most of those reasons are actually symptoms of a greater problem.

The root problem is time focused on other areas, instead of on our families. Sometimes we are even so focused on our spiritual lives that we aren't paying attention to our family life.

Let's talk about fatherhood. Many fathers are absent from the home today. They are not involved in the lives of their families. In some communities 70% of babies are born out of wedlock with no father in the home. Add to that families where the dads are in the home but he is so busy with his career that he is not paying attention or involved.

I would suggest that if you have goals in the areas of your business, finance, and career you should also have goals in the area of your family life. You should take time to plan for what you really want your family to look like. Do you have goals for how you are going to pass your values on to your children? Do you have a specific plan of action for how your sons will learn to become men of honor? Do you have a plan for how your daughters will grow into true ladies—Proverbs 31 women?

How about your marriage? If you want to stay married, you need a plan of action. Good marriages just don't happen. What goals do you have for your marriage?

The questions in this chapter are designed to help you show the most important people in your life how much you care about them. By simply making a plan and setting aside time to do it, you will ensure that your commitment to your family remains the priority it ought to be. You probably would not be reading this book if you did not already have family as one of your most important priorities. However, I'd like to suggest that unless you are careful, other priorities in your life can easily creep in and cause you to neglect time with your family. Even though you love them and desire to serve them, unless you have a plan of action and stick to it, you may wake up one day and realize it is too late.

A good friend of mine once told me that my fear of loss in business was actually going to create my greatest loss of all if I did not make some changes. He saw how hard I was working, taking every speaking engagement I could get so I would not miss any opportunity to reach people. He pointed out that because of my fear of losing opportunities to do what I love and further my career, I was actually missing precious time with my children that I would never be able to get back.

He was right. I was so glad he cared enough to point out the imbalance that was creeping into my life. He reminded me what it was going to cost me and I made some immediate changes.

Family is extremely important to me. For Kara and me, our number one priority is making sure that our children are raised in a loving home and prepared for their lives. I would not take another speaking engagement if my family needed me to be home 24/7 for any reason.

I am very passionate about my work because saving freedom for my family is very important to me. But it is very easy for me to get so caught up in the things I am doing *for* my family that I miss spending time *with* them. If I miss being a part of their lives, then my Actual Values have become something very different from my Desired Values.

When my friend pointed out the risk of such a great loss, I found that family was number one and two on my desired values list, but were number six and seven on my actual values list. I had to do the work to change that because I only have so much time with my kids, and I do not want to wake up one day and realize it is too late.

During my first session in the legislature I was gone so much that my son Trey, who was about three at the time, walked out to the car with me one morning and said, *"Daddy please don't go to the capital again because I'm going to miss you!"* I cried all the way to the capitol because I realized I was not going to get these days of him being that young back. I realized I needed more balance in my life.

Obviously, fathers cannot stay home 24/7 with their kids. Somebody has to go out and make a living and that is chiefly a dad's role. The goal is to keep some balance in our lives so we do not get too caught up in career or any other area, and then miss the important moments with our kids.

We only have so much time.

It's the same with your spouse, parents, and with every other member of your family. As you go through the following questions, write some specific things down that you want to do with each of them before they are gone or before you are gone. If it's not part of your life plan and your purpose, it's not going to happen. It doesn't happen by accident, so be purposeful and start planning now!

1. What are you planning to do special for or with your grandparents before they pass on in life?

2. What are you planning to do special for or with your parents before they pass on in life?

3. How does the concept of marriage fit into your life?

4. If you could have the perfect spouse or loving relationship, what would it be like? (Keep in mind a realistic balance)

5. What are you expecting most out of your relationship with your spouse?

6. How does the concept of a family fit into your life?

7. If you could have the perfect family life, what would it be like?

8. What are you expecting most out of your relationship with your family?

9. What special thing can you do for each member of your family this week?

19

MENTAL

In this chapter, you will be looking closely at the mental aspects of your life in terms of intelligence, education, and how you process information. You will be working on learning strategies and answering questions that will help you identify the most important things you have ever learned.

I firmly believe the day you stop learning is the day you start growing stagnant and your dreams and goals begin to die. If you stop learning, the rest of your life will be a mere existence. In order to live your purpose, you must be constantly growing and improving. This chapter will help you to develop ways you can do that.

If you are not a speed-reader, you might want to learn how so you can take in more information. It's easy to do, just get a good course. One of my first businesses was teaching a speed-reading course.

You could also take a memory course, learn a foreign language, take up a new sport, or teach a Bible study. Every time you force yourself to stretch in some way, your identity grows, your talents multiply, and God will use you in ways you never dreamed possible.

The questions in this chapter will help you assess your learning strategy. Some people are visual learners, some are auditory learners, and some learn best kinesthetically. I am a visual learner, which means I take in information best when I see it on paper or watch it in a video. If I listen, I do not learn it as well. Visual learners do not remember much of what they hear. If I meet someone new and that person tells me his or her name, it is very difficult for me to remember it. But, if they are wearing a nametag, I'm much more likely to remember it. The visual aspects help me to learn.

You may not be a visual learner. You may be an auditory learner, which means that you will learn new things a lot better by listening to CD's or MP3s than you would by reading it in a book. You should probably always be listening to an audiobook, so that you can be learning new things every day.

Kinesthetic means you actually need to be doing it. You are a hands-on learner. The workbook section of this book will be very helpful for you, because you will be doing the activity rather than just thinking about it. If you go through the exercises at the end of each chapter, you will learn a lot faster.

The goal is to discover your best learning strategy and start using it. If you are an auditory learner, use audiobooks. If you are a visual learner, read or watch

DVDs. If you are a kinesthetic learner, start doing the activities while you are learning. Whatever your learning strategy is, spend time improving your mental capacity. If you give up an hour of TV in return for taking on some new challenge, you will be constantly growing and improving.

If possible, go to seminars that will help you to improve your skills. You may not like everything in a seminar or a book, but look for those golden nuggets that you can glean that will help you. Start adding them to your toolbox.

In the questions that follow, you will be asked how many books per year are you going to read, and what will be the books. I think this is one of the most important questions. Take the time to list out the books that you'd like to read over the next month, year, etc. I have a three-year reading plan. I may not get to them as fast as I want, and sometimes I have to replace them with a new book that is more important, but having a plan helps you to begin to chip away and get the knowledge you want to acquire. This is a very important step in living your purpose.

1. What time each day will you set aside to read, review, and refine your Living Your Purpose book?

2. How would you describe your most healthy mental life?

3. What are five of the most important things you have ever learned?

    1.

    2.

    3.

    4.

    5.

4. How fast would you like to read? What speed-reading course will you take?

5. How many books per year are you going to read? List the next ten books you will read and dates by which you will finish reading them:

    1.

    2.

    3.

    4.

    5.

6. What languages would you love to learn and be fluent in? How and when do you intend to do so?

7. What is your most effective process for learning? Reading, viewing, listening, doing, or all?

It would be wise to discover your personal learning strategy and discover ways to effectively take in more information and remember it.

VISUAL LEARNERS:

1. Remember what they read and write.

2. Focus in on the visual part of a presentation (they LOVE PowerPoint and handouts). Speakers and teachers who do not distribute handouts or use slides during a speech are missing the best opportunity to get their message across to the 40% of the audience who are typically visual learners and will not "hear" much of the speech any way.

3. Understand best when they can SEE the information!

4. Prefer a time-line or other similar diagram to remember historical events.

5. Prefer written instructions rather than verbal instructions.

6. Prefer photographs and illustrations with printed content.

7. Remember and understand through the use of diagrams, charts, and maps.

Learning Strategies for the Visual Learner:

1. Write down things you want to remember

2. Look at the person who is speaking to you; it will help you focus.

3. Get a study partner that takes good notes in class!

4. When studying, take many notes and write down lots of details.

5. When trying to learn material by writing notes, cover your notes then re-write. Re-writing will help you remember. Do this with your speeches too.

6. Use color to highlight main ideas.

7. Try to put your desk away from the door and windows and close to the front of the class.

8. Make flashcards. Look at them often and write out the main points, then check.

9. Where possible, use charts, maps, posters, films, videos, computer software, etc.

AUDITORY LEARNERS

1. Remember what they hear and say. They remember oral instructions well.

2. Enjoy classroom and small-group discussion.

Learning Strategies for the Auditory Learner

1. Study with a friend so you can talk about the information and HEAR it, too.

2. Recite the information that you want to remember out loud, several times.

3. Make your own recordings of important points you want to remember and listen to them, repeatedly. This is especially useful for learning material for tests or memorizing speeches.

4. When reading, skim through and look at the pictures, chapter titles, and other clues. Say out loud what you think this book could be about.

5. Make flashcards for the material you want to learn and use them repeatedly, reading them out loud.

6. Read out loud when possible. You need to HEAR the words as you read them to understand them well.

KINESTHETIC LEARNERS

1. Remember things they experience, what they DO with their hands and bodies (movement and touch).

2. Enjoy using tools or lessons, which involve active and practical participation.

3. Have great motor memory. They can remember how to do things after they've done them only once.

Learning Strategies for the Kinesthetic Learner

1. To memorize, pace or walk around while reciting to yourself or using flashcards or notes.

2. When reading a short story or chapter in a book, try a whole-to-part approach. This means you should first scan the pictures, then read headings, then read the first and last paragraphs and try to get a feel for the book. You could also try skim reading the chapter or short story backwards, paragraph-by-paragraph.

3. If you need to fidget, try jiggling your legs or feet, hand or finger exercises; handle a koosh ball, tennis ball or something similar.

4. You might not study best while at a desk. Try lying on your stomach or back. Try studying while sitting in a comfortable lounge chair or on cushions or a beanbag.

20

PHYSICAL

Honesty is important, so I have to be honest with you about this chapter. On my balance sheet, this is one area where I never score off the charts. I have to admit, the physical aspect of my life is challenging. I also have to remind myself that my body is the temple of God.

I find inspiration from reading about King Solomon and the temple he built in the Old Testament. His father, King David, gave all of his personal fortune to Solomon for the building project. Many of the Israelites did the same. The entire inside of the temple was covered in pure gold and decorated with precious stones. The curtains made of the finest, beautifully colored linens. Massive carved pillars were placed on the outside. A twenty foot solid bronze alter was constructed, along with a golden lampstand, sprinkling bowls, and a number of other intricate items that filled the interior. It was a magnificent temple that would be worth millions of dollars today.

Imagine if you could travel back in time and behold the splendor of it all. Do you think you would go into that place with mud on your shoes, or that you would leave your trash inside? You would never open a carton of eggs and start throwing them against the altar or the pillars.

Of course not! You would never consider treating God's temple that way.

Where is God's temple today? The Bible teaches that today His Spirit resides in the bodies of believers. We are His temple! Our physical bodies are miraculously made, not by the hands of men as King Solomon's temple was, but by the mighty hand of God. Each of us are physical miracles. If we consider it for a moment, we will realize that our bodies are much more impressive and worth far more than that massive structure built by Solomon. The intricate detail and sheer miraculous workings of the human body are amazing.

You have a billion dollar body; if you don't believe me, take an inventory.

When I was in law school, we studied several personal injury cases. One multimillion dollar settlement was for the lose of eyesight. Another was a person who lost an arm and received a multi-million dollar settlement. Another received two million for the loss of his legs. What about the value of a brain, heart, or any other organs?

Put it all together and you realize that you are literally a walking, talking, breathing, billion-dollar miracle, built by God!

So if would not walk into the temple of Solomon and trash it, how much more respect should we have for our body—the temple of the living God. I am not suggesting that you worship your body, or that it becomes so important to you that you get out of balance in other areas of your life. All I'm suggesting is that we ought to respect the bodies God has given us. We ought to take good physical care of ourselves, as best we can.

As I confessed already, this area is a challenge for me. This is probably my weakest of the seven areas. I struggle with it. I have to tell you, jogging on a treadmill makes me feel like a hamster on a wheel because I feel like I am putting out a lot of energy and getting absolutely nowhere! I've set some goals in the last couple of years and gotten better. I cut out soft drinks and sweets, but I still do not work out nearly enough and there are a lot of other things I need to be doing better.

Go through each of the following questions. Establish some good, reasonable goals. Consistently come back to measure and adjust so that you can reach those goals. If you take good care of your body, you are going to have more vitality and be much more effective in the other areas of your life as well.

1. How would you currently rate your physical health?

2. What changes would you like to make to your physical health?

3. What must you do to make those changes?

4. When will you make them?

5. If you live to be 100, what will you have done to take care of your physical body so that your vitality and health are optimum?

6. What physical activities do you plan on doing over the next five years?

7. Who is the longest living person you know or have met?

8. What do you believe the secret to their longevity is?

9. What specifically do you plan on doing to keep your body well?

10. How many hours do you plan on sleeping each day?

21

FINANCIAL

You are now going to be looking at the financial aspect of your life. You will notice that in order of importance, I do not rank this area as high as spiritual, family, physical, or mental. Those areas ought to come first in priority. But the financial side of life is obviously important too.

Many people have some interesting money myths that they have held most of their lives. Think about any of the myths you have about money and take time to write them down as you work through this chapter. These myths are limiting beliefs. Perhaps you have already listed them in the chapter covering your beliefs.

For our purposes now, work on any money myths you have adopted over the years, and start getting detailed about what changes you would like to make in your finances.

What are your financial goals?

Some people believe that money IS the root of all evil, but it's actually not. The Bible tells us in 1 Timothy

6:10 that it is the LOVE of money that is the root of all evil. Money itself is not the issue, it's what people do for money and with it that causes problems in our world. This misunderstanding has been one of the most commonly believed distortions of recent generations.

It is possible that this verse from Paul's first letter to Timothy has been misquoted more than any other verse in Scripture. Many people have taught, either directly or insinuated through undertone, that financial success is an evil tool of Satan. The innuendos are usually more deadly to believers than the direct pronouncements because it kills any natural ambition or drive they may have to be financially successful.

A very common undertone prevalent in the Christian world is the attitude that if you are extremely successful financially, you must be living in sin. It is automatically assumed that along the way, you must have cheated someone, stolen, or taken advantage of some little old ladies, in order to get ahead.

Of course the liberals in Congress are just as bad. They always blame those who are financially successful. Accusing them of stealing from starving children or destroying the environment to get their wealth. In their minds, if by some rare chance you managed to earn money without doing anything immoral or illegal, the only honorable thing to do with that money is to give it all to government. These self-righteous liberals act as if you are sinful if you decide to keep any of your own money. They cannot stand it when other people succeed. Yet these same characters of hypocrisy tithe less and give less to charity than any other group of Americans.

The truth is, the image of wealth as evil is derived 0% from the Bible and 100% from jealousy. Unfortunately, when we humans see someone else with something we wish we had, it is a common knee jerk reaction of our flesh to condemn it. Remember how we worked on that in an earlier chapter. Don't do that!

Disdain for successful individuals has a lot to do with our own insecurities and very little to do with the moral character of the successful individual in question. Remember, money is not the root of all evil. It is the LOVE of money that is the root of all evil.

The object itself, money, has no moral impact. It is the character of the person, in this case, his or her love of the object of money that has an effect. Without question, if you become so consumed with money that the other priorities in your life suffer, especially God and family, then money has become an idol in your life, and that is sin. And no matter how much money you have, money alone will never make you happy.

I know plenty of extremely wealthy people who have no joy. They are not happy because their love of money has cost them dearly in their marriages, their relationships with their children, their spiritual lives, and every other area as well. You do not want to go down that path.

But at the same time, you do not want to do the opposite either. You do not want to hate money or fall for the lie that an inanimate object, such as money, can somehow control you.

We live in a world where money is important, so we need to know how to relate to it in a healthy way. The Bible speaks about those who manage their money well. In the parable of the talents in Matthew 25, we learn that those servants who actually managed their money well turned it into more and were rewarded for doing so.

That is a good thing. We need to learn to do the same. We need good financial goals and a clear picture of how our finances fit within our purpose. Again, it's not the most important priority in our lives, but it is an important aspect that we can learn to use in a way that will help us to live our purpose.

When Paul talked about the love of money being the root of all kinds of evil, clearly he put the responsibility for the use of money in our hands, not in the object. The power is not in money—it is in our hands. How we use money is what matters. This is an action on our part requiring decisions, emotions, and human rational. The love of money is not referring to a deep affection for the pieces of paper with deceased patriots' photos on them. It is referring to our desire for and use of the object, and where it ranks on our list of priorities.

If your rich uncle passed away tomorrow and left you $100 million, would you be in sin simply because you now posses that money? Of course not! You are not accountable for the fact that the money was left to you. You are only accountable for what you do with it after you get it. If that money becomes your God and rules you, instead of you ruling it, then clearly you have a love of money problem and it's going to cause you all kinds of grief, just as Paul talked about in 1 Timothy 6.

I do not believe it is God's plan for everybody to be rich, but don't allow a fear that you might allow money to control you, to cause you to refuse God's financial blessings. If you are faithful in managing what He gives, He just might allow you to have much more. Some are not good money managers because they can't handle the temptations that come with it. If that is you, then I hope God does not bless you financially, unless you can learn how to handle it better.

Regardless of where you are today, financially, it makes sense to start working on some good strategies that will help you become a better steward of whatever blessings the Lord wants to give you.

A movie that was out a long time ago, called Congo, was about a diamond mine in the jungle that had been cultivated by an evil business owner. (Of course, the capitalist had to be evil, that's Hollyweird for you.) He was a really bad guy and created a way to use the diamonds for some weird, futuristic telecommunications devise. The screenwriters transferred his personal evil onto the lifeless objects in question, the diamonds, and suddenly the diamonds themselves were cursed. In the closing scene of this absurd movie, the main characters are escaping the jungle in a hot air balloon. The star of the movie still has one of these extremely large diamond and he throws the diamond over the side of the hot air balloon as some ridiculous victory over the evil lure of wealth.

Common sense is not something we often find in Hollyweird. Instead of tossing a valuable diamond, why not keep it and use it for good? Wouldn't that have been a better ending? In real life, that diamond would have been worth millions. Just because someone was less than ethical in using it, does that make the inanimate, lifeless object evil? Does it make sense to throw away that wealth? It would have been better if that person would have used the diamond for good.

Often we do the same thing with our own finances. Because others have allowed money to control them, or they have used wealth in an evil way, we transfer their morality to the inanimate object. The problem with that thinking is that inanimate objects have no morals. You are the one who determines how an object will be used, whether for good or evil.

So, if you wake up one day with $100 million left to you by that rich uncle, do not throw it overboard from your hot air balloon! Find out how God wants you to use it and be a faithful steward of His money. If you don't have a rich uncle who might leave you $100 million, why not ask God how you can create some wealth in this wonderful free enterprise system we have in America?

It's actually a silly argument to say that money is evil. After all, isn't it true that God owns all the wealth? Whether it is in the form of gold or silver, paper with pictures of deceased notables, or the cattle on a thousand hills, He owns it all. If all the wealth is God's and wealth is evil, wouldn't that make God rather evil?

The bottom line is this, you can use whatever money you have to bless other people. I'm not saying you have to be rich. Not at all! You've just got to work through your priorities. Finances may play a smaller role in your purpose than in others. This is *your* life plan, so it depends on the desires God placed in your heart.

Go through this section on finances and set some good goals and think through what you realistically would like to see in your life, financially, and begin to live your purpose in this area as well.

1. What money myths do you hold? Examples: 'Money is bad.' 'Wealthy people are unhappy.' 'Wealthy people are dishonest.' 'It is better to give than to receive.' 'I can't afford it.'

2. Is it money you would like to earn more of or is it what money can buy?

3. What organizations (churches, non-profits, political,

candidates, etc.) would you bless financially if you achieved financial abundance?

4. How do you define financial abundance?

5. Is "freedom" worth living below your means so that you can contribute 5% to 10% of your income to causes and organizations working to protect your freedom?

6. Describe the dream car(s) that would meet your needs without being wasteful?

7. If money were not an issue, describe your dream home while thinking about being a good steward of what the Lord Blesses you with. What would it look like? How many rooms would it have? Name them. How is it decorated? How is it landscaped? What kind of furniture? What else would you love to have in your dream home? What is your dream home address? (Anywhere in the world)

8. What are your dream clothes? The way you dress will impact

the way you and others feel about you. Others will treat you the way you are perceived to be treating yourself.

9. How would you love to look?

10. If you could have one dream wish come true what would it be?

11. What does your dream day consist of? (break it down hour by hour)

12. What would be your perfect vacation?

13. It is wise to spend time dreaming. Pursue your own dreams, not someone else's. Be sure the ideal is balanced with the real. Write down some more dreams items you know you would love to possess.

14. If time and money were no object, what else would you love to do and have?

15. What would be your ideal way of making money?

16. How many hours would you love to work?

22

CAREER

As you identify your passion and learn to live your purpose, you could find that your career might change. If you do not really love what you are doing, and it is not part of your purpose, then you may want to look for a way out of what you are currently doing and find a way into those things that you would truly love doing.

The questions in this chapter are designed to help you think about how you can get into an area that you truly love. What is a career that you would be talented in? What are your strengths? How could they be used where you can grow?

Maybe you are in that place right now. I pray that you are. If so, my hope is that this process will serve to reinforce that purpose and cause you to gain a new passion for what you are doing.

1. What would you love to do for a Career?

2. What is your concise definition of Success? Sample: *"Success is living my purpose and having a positive impact on others, while living with congruency and integrity."*

3. What three things that you have accomplished are you the most inspired about?

4. What three CAREER objectives would you most love to accomplish?

5. What would you do if you knew you couldn't fail?

6. If you could succeed in any career, what profession or occupation or business would you love to be in?

7. In what profession/occupation/business do you currently spend the most time?

8. In what profession/occupation/business are you most talented?

9. In what career talent or strength are you most gifted?

10. In what profession/occupation/business would you love to be an expert?

11. What would it take for you to become an expert in that field?

12. Are you willing to invest 10,000 hours into becoming an expert in that field?

23

COMMUNITY

Some use the word *social* for this particular area of life. I use the word *community* because it reminds me that as important as my family and my church are to me, I am also part of a larger community and there are important relationships there as well.

In this chapter of your life plan, you will spend some time thinking about those community relationships. There are lots of fun questions to answer and work through as you think about your involvement in the community at large, and with people in your life beyond your family.

There are some powerful activities to spend some time on towards the end of this chapter. Don't jump ahead, because you are going to go through some basic questions beforehand. These questions will be about who you would like to form relationships with, some heroes that you would like to meet, etc.

I remember setting out twenty years ago to meet a lot of people that I had considered my heroes at the time. I wanted to interview them and spend time with them and I was able to do that as part of a project I created. I was able to build relationships with men I admired and wanted to learn from, such as Zig Ziglar, Tony Robbins, and Dick Cheney. It was a great experience for me. Not because I am into hero worship, but because I wanted to learn from them and ask them questions.

You can do the same.

In this chapter you will also think through some of the things in your community that you would like to be a part of. Are there any organizations that you believe make a positive difference? What can you do to support them? Maybe there is a cause that you are passionate about, but there is no organization working on that cause. What has to happen for you to start such an organization? You will then make a specific list of three things you can do this year to serve and improve your community.

You will also make a list of all of your key relationships, including those people who are part of your various teams, whether your career team, family team, work out partners, whoever it might be. Next to each person's name, you will make a list of creative ways you can show them that you care about them. Then, you will set a date for doing it.

For instance, if it is your workout partner or trainer, what is something special you can do for them? Is there a gift you could get for them that would let them know how much you appreciate them helping to make you better physically?

Maybe one of those key relationships is an employee or employer or co-worker. Find some way, it does not have to be expensive or extravagant, that you can show them you care about them and appreciate them. Obviously, every member of your family falls into that category. Find ways to let people know how much you appreciate them.

Then you will spend time thinking about relationships that may need repairing. Maybe it is someone you need to forgive. They might not even still be alive, but you harbor bitterness towards them for something that happened in the past. If so, then you are currently paying a price for that lack of forgiveness. I want to encourage you to write a letter of forgiveness to that person. If they are still living, decide later whether or not you actually want to deliver it to them.

I had a situation once where I had a nasty fight with a political opponent. It was incredibly painful for my family. I will not go into how ruthless it was, and the dirty tricks that were played. It was awful. I harbored a lot of resentment. Not for the way the election turned out, but for the pain that we went through and the ugliness with which the campaign was fought. I had a lot of resentment. Did I already say that? By the way, did I mention that I harbored a lot of resentment? You get the idea!

Months later, I thought I had let it go and forgiven, but I learned that I actually had not. The Bible talks about not letting bitterness take root, but I had let it take root.

Several months after the election I was working with my friend David Barton at his ranch, and somehow this former opponent's name came up. I guess there was something in my response and facial expression that revealed the bitterness in my heart. David's daughter, Damaris went into another room and returned with a book. She handed it to me and said, *"You need to read this."*

It was *Total Forgiveness*, by R. T. Kindel. That book radically changed my thinking. It helped me finally let go of the bitterness that was tearing me down and hurting me.

Find ways to give forgiveness and also to seek forgiveness. Maybe there is someone you've wronged. We humans do that. We make mistakes. Don't let another day go by without taking steps towards sincerely apologizing to someone that you have wronged. If you have committed a wrong, admit it, and seek reconciliation. You may not get the response you would like. That person may choose not to forgive you. Only your apology is within your power, their forgiveness is not up to you. Write that letter and then decide later whether or not you will deliver it.

As I mentioned, it may be someone who is no longer alive. I would encourage you to still write the letter and seek or give forgiveness, whichever the situation is for you. My guess is there will be a little bit of both. It certainly was for me the first time that I went through this process.

Then of course, lastly, communicate your love and appreciation for anyone in your life that you have not told. It's time to find a way to do it. What if you found yourself on your deathbed tomorrow? Lord willing, that is not going to happen; but if it did, would you wish that you had written all these letters?

Don't wait. Do it now.

1. If you could have the perfect community contacts or friends, what would they be like?

2. If you could have the perfect community life, what would it be like?

3. Who are your seven top community heroes?

4. What five non-celebrities would you love to meet? When?

5. What top ten celebrities would you love to meet?

6. How do you plan or imagine yourself meeting them?

7. What three questions would you love to ask them?

8. If you could correspond with any person in the world who would that be?

9. What organizations do you believe make a positive difference in your community, state and/or nation? What can you do to support those organizations?

10. Is there a cause about which you are passionate, but there is no organization working on the cause?

11. What would have to happen for you to start such an organization?

12. What three things will you do this year to serve and improve your community?

13. Make a list of all your key relationships. Next to each person's name, list creative ways that you can let him or her know you care about them and set a date for doing it.

14. GIVING FORGIVENESS. Is there anyone you need to forgive? Perhaps they are living or dead, but if there is a person towards whom you still harbor bitterness or resentment, then you are paying a price for that lack of forgiveness and the healing can take place as soon as you take action. Take time now to write a letter of forgiveness to that person and decide later whether or not to deliver it.

15. SEEKING FORGIVENESS. Is there someone from whom you need to seek forgiveness? Don't let another day go by without taking steps towards sincerely apologizing for a wrong you have committed. Reconciliation may never occur and the person may choose not to forgive you. Those things are outside your control. But the apology is entirely within your power. Take time now to write a letter of apology to that person (or persons) and decide later whether or not to deliver it.

16. COMMUNICATING LOVE AND APPRECIATION. Is there anyone in your life that you love and appreciate, but have perhaps not communicated that love and appreciation to very well?

If you found yourself on your deathbed tomorrow, would you

wish you had written these letters? Don't wait, do it now.

17. What national landmarks would you like to visit? When will you visit them?

18. What countries would you love to learn about and visit? How and when do you intend to do so?

19. If you could solve one community problem, what would it be?

20. What community cause are you dedicating your life too?

21. What community impact do you plan on making?

22. What influence or legacy do you plan on leaving?

23. What community leadership roles do you plan to take on?

24. What community service do you believe you can provide most?

25. What community events, parties, clubs or groups do you plan on socializing at? When?

26. How would your best friend describe you to someone who didn't know you?

27. What would you love Time Magazine to write about you in twenty years?

28. Go to a travel agent and ask for a copy of every brochure they have. Cut out the pictures of all the locations in the world you would love to visit. What cultures and places would you love

to visit? If you could travel anywhere you would love, where would it be?

29. What would have to happen for you to take your family on an RV trip around the nation before the kids are too old to enjoy it?

30. What would be the ultimate trip with which you could surprise your spouse?

24

CLOSING THOUGHTS

I do not want to say we are coming to the end, because as I've said throughout this book, this is an ongoing process. So, my prayer is that you will constantly come back to this Living Your Purpose workbook and go through each section again and again and again. If you are going to do this effectively, you will spend time going through parts of it every day.

The idea is to make this your own book. Take each of these sections and own them, adjust them, change them, delete them, move them around to where it fits your life.

There are a few items that we have not yet covered. These are topics that could certainly be part of earlier chapters, but I wanted you to not go through them until you had completed the rest of the chapters and were better able to define your purpose and your goals.

Think of these items as an appendix and work on them after you have completed all of the workbook sections from earlier chapters. Each of these need to be typed into your computer, preferably the digital version of the Living Your Purpose workbook and then reworked on a continual basis.

Appendix A - Speaking Introduction

This is an appendix to the material we covered earlier on identity (Chapters 1-4). Even if you think you may never need a speaking introduction, taking time to craft one will help you to better define yourself. How would you like to be introduced to a group?

If speaking in front of a group is something you do now or will be doing, you would also find the Leaders Edge program titled, *The Power of Purposeful Communication*, a helpful resource. As a leader, you are going to end up in front of a group (big or small) at some point, teaching and sharing your ideas. Preparing a speaking introduction allows you to think, ahead of time, about what you would like to have said about you by the person who will be introducing you. What information could he or she share that would give you credibility in front of the group?

Work on your speaking introduction, refining it over time and you will have it ready for the day when you will be invited to speak. More importantly, working on it now will help you develop confidence in that particular area of your identity.

Appendix B - Biography

This is also an appendix to the chapters on identity (Chapters 1-4). Write a biography that describes your life, *as you want it to be lived.* This is something that you will come back to and add your new accomplishments to, so that you have it all in one place. Essentially, this is the condensed story of your life that could be read in a quick biography.

Appendix C – Calendar Goals

The last few pages consist of three specific lists of goals that you can begin to set in your life. These lists are an appendix to the goals chapter (chapter 15).

One of the lists is titled *Yearly Goals - My Purpose in 2014.* This is a place where you can begin listing all of your goals for this particular year under the specific areas of your life. It may be up to three or four pages long. This is an opportunity for you to see everything you hope to accomplish by the end of this year, in one place.

It does not necessarily mean you are going to accomplish everything you have on your list. As time goes by, you may realize that you have to move some of those things to 2015 because you just are not going to get there or some other things have come up in your life that you need to get done first. Don't let that bother you, your list is not written in stone. Remember, you are working on fulfilling God's will and plan for your life and that will be accomplished in His timing, which is not always going to be the same as your timeline. The purpose of these lists is to get all your goals down in one place so you can get started. There are three lists that I'm encouraging you to create:

1. **Yearly Goals** – Create one for each year (i.e., My Purpose in 2014, My Purpose in 2015, etc.)

2. **Monthly Goals** – Create one for each month (i.e, My Purpose in January 2013). Take your yearly goals and break them down to what you would like to see happen on a monthly basis. It helps you to see the progress of each of those goals.

3. **Weekly Goals** – Create one for each week, (i.e., My Purpose this Week, January 5-11, 2014.) Take your monthly goals and break them down to what you would like to see happen on a weekly basis. You can plan approximately three to six weeks in advance.

In the end you will have an annual plan, twelve monthly plans, and three to six weekly plans. That will help you to take every goal you would like to accomplish and break it down into bite-size pieces that you can accomplish, literally on a daily basis.

You can use a simple sheet of paper or note page in your computer, or you may prefer to put them into your calendar. Personally, I do both. I open up the calendar to see what I have for that day, but I also like to see my goals for the whole year in one place and that's hard to do in most calendars. Using a one-page summary helps me to see the big picture and to break it down into more manageable pieces, on a weekly, monthly, and yearly basis. Now that we have the Living Your Purpose digital workbook, it's easy to keep all of this in one place without any paper!

As you develop your life plan, you will learn what works best for you. You do not have to do everything the way I do it. I hope I have given you some golden nuggets. These are the things that I have learned from others along the way that you can pick and chose from to create your own life plan.

Keep coming back and working through your plan, try to get completely through it every couple of weeks. The more consistent you are, the better you will stay on track with the goals you have set. I've found that whenever I've missed extended periods of time away from daily reviewing my Life Plan, I always get off track.

So be consistent, be disciplined. You've done a lot of work to create this plan for yourself, so it makes sense to keep up the maintenance. If you come back to your life plan repeatedly, you will live your purpose.

We have certainly been given much opportunity in America and the Bible says to whom much is given, much is required. I'm exhorting you to make the most of the freedom, opportunities, and skills that God has given you.

Live the purposes He has for your life.

The real American dream is not a life of ease and excess, with little thought or care for the future. Don't get deceived by all those advertisements that tell you the reward for a hard day's work is to drink beer all night and watch endless commercials that will entice you to buy things you can't afford.

I believe in an American Dream that says you can be a blessing to others. You can go out there and be used by God. Don't sit around waiting for life to happen to you, get busy and enjoy the life you have been given. Live it to the fullest.

The real American dream for a true child of God is to live your purpose with great passion and joy. You've got one life to give, for what will you give your one life?

Seize each day for all it's worth because before you know it, today will be over. You only have one today. What will you do with it? What will you do with this life that God has given you?

When I was in high school one of my friends was killed in a car accident. It was tragic, but it made me realize what a privilege it is to wake up in the morning. Some folks did not wake up this morning, and they will never get a chance to live another day. Their opportunity to live for something that matters is over. You did wake up this morning, so that means you still have your one life to give.

What are you going to do with it today?

A year from now, five years from now, will you be able to look back and say, I did my best to give my life in a way that matters, that impacted others. Jack London said, "*I would rather be a superb meteor, every atom in me a magnificent glow, then a sleepy and permanent planet. The proper function of man is to live, not to exist. I shall not waste my days in trying to prolong them. I shall use my time.*" George Bernard Shaw wrote an excellent wake up call for all of us when he said, "*I want to be thoroughly used up when I die, for the harder I work, the more I live. I rejoice in life, for it's own sake. Life is no brief candle; to me it is a splendid torch. One that I've got hold of for the moment and I want to hold it high and let it burn as brightly as possible before passing it on to future generations.*"

How bright will the torch of your life burn? What will you do with your talents, ambitions, and desires? I encourage you to use it now. Do not wait until you think the timing is perfect. Take action now and keep taking action until you get the results you are after. Allow your goals and dreams to fuel your passion. Live your life to the fullest. God has given you a purpose, He's given you passion, now it is up to you to go and live your purpose.

ABOUT THE AUTHOR...

Rick is a former Texas State Representative, attorney, author, and nationally recognized speaker on the Constitution and America's founding principles. He currently co-hosts the daily radio talk show *WallBuilders Live! w/David Barton*. Rick and his wife, Kara, and their children travel the Nation together teaching on the Constitution and inspiring citizens to do their part in protecting our cherished freedoms. They bring history to life with their fun and entertaining adventures in their *Chasing American Legends* reality television series.

Connect with the Green family at RickGreen.com for regular updates, articles, and liberty inspiring information!